Steam Routes around
—CHELTENHAM—

and

TEWKESBURY • WINCHCOMBE • ANDOVERSFORD

Busy times at Cloddy bridge, 15 June 1961. WD 2-8-0 No.90137 from Woodford Halse shed brings a mixed goods north – probably going back to its home on the old Great Central line between Banbury and Rugby – while No.5046 *Earl Cawdor* speeds along on the up *Cornishman*. On the down relief line is No. 4930 *Hagley Hall* on a van train.   *J. Dagley-Morris*

© Stephen Mourton October 1993

ISBN 1 870754 28 X

Printed by The Amadeus Press Ltd, Huddersfield, West Yorkshire

**RUNPAST PUBLISHING
CHELTENHAM**

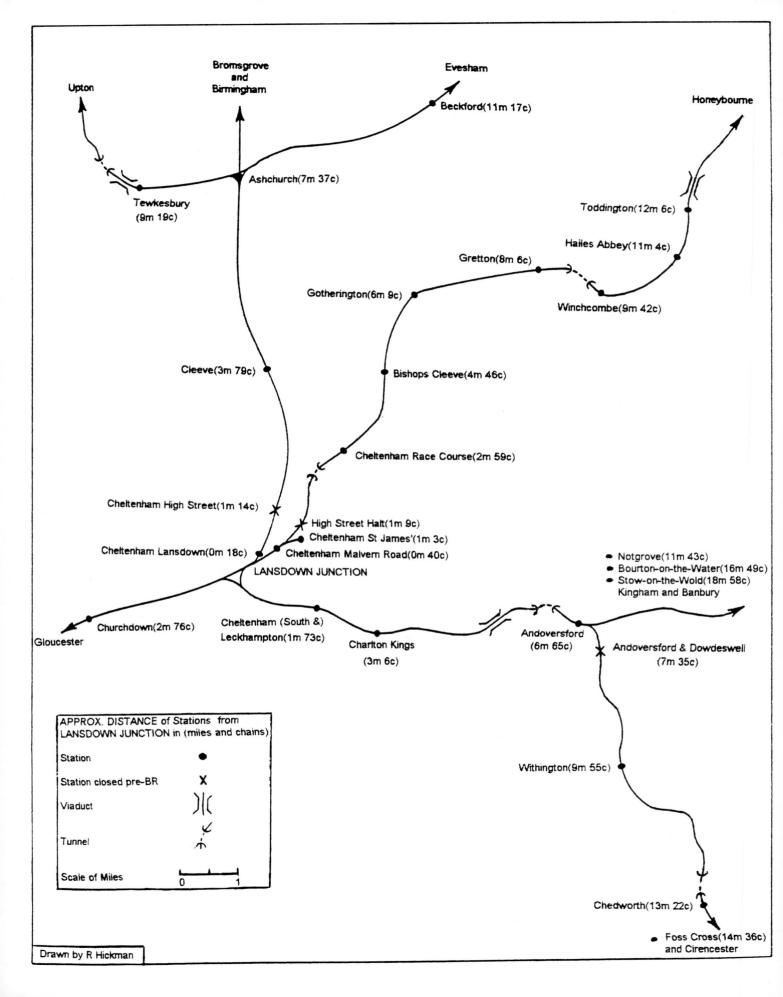

INTRODUCTION

A number of railway books over the years have included Cheltenham, but coverage has usually been combined with the Cotswolds, the rest of Gloucestershire or with very detailed histories of lines in the area. So it was thought fitting to compile this mainly pictorial book about Cheltenham itself and the surrounding district.

Cheltenham was not a major railway centre in steam days like, say, Swindon or Derby, and, for enthusiasts, was overshadowed by nearby Gloucester, with its large engine sheds and goods yards, but the sheer volume of traffic and variety of motive power, from all the Big Four railway companies, made it a fascinating place to observe trains. Indeed, such was the local enthusiasm that one of the enduring railway societies, the Railway Correspondence and Travel Society (RCTS), was founded in Cheltenham many years ago.

This book's brief historical survey of railways in the area shows that, because of its strategic location, routes through Cheltenham were very much sought after by various companies, following on from stagecoaches, which had also regarded the town as an important stopping point. In turn, the railways no doubt helped the development of Cheltenham as an important centre of education and tourism. The railway map of the area took over one hundred years to complete, from the arrival of the Birmingham and Gloucester in 1840 to the widening to four tracks between Cheltenham and Gloucester in 1942.

The book also covers the area around the neighbouring country junctions at Ashchurch, with its rare flat crossing on a main line, and the rather tranquil Andoversford, where the impudent and impecunious Midland & South Western Junction Railway attempted to compete with the mighty Great Western Railway.

I have tried to use previously unpublished material in the pictorial survey; this has not always been possible, but hopefully reproduction of photographs seen before is, in most cases, much better, and has considerably enhanced their interest.

Stephen Mourton, Cheltenham, September 1993

CONTENTS

Historical Survey:	Page
Gloucester & Cheltenham Tramroad	5
Birmingham & Gloucester Railway	5
Routes around Ashchurch	6
Cheltenham & Great Western Union Railway	7
Banbury & Cheltenham Direct Railway	9
Midland & South Western Junction Railway	9
Great Western Railway – Cheltenham to Honeybourne	11
Widening between Cheltenham and Gloucester	11
Traffic Flows	12
Motive Power	14
Pictorial Survey:	
Churchdown and Badgeworth	19
Hatherley and Reddings	24
Cloddymore Crossing	29
Lansdown Junction	32
Towards Andoversford Junction	35
Leckhampton	36
Charlton Kings	37
Around Andoversford	41
Towards Kingham	43

	Page
Bourton-on-the-Water	44
Stow-on-the-Wold	45
On The MSWJ	46
Foss Cross	49
Lansdown Station	50
Malvern Road	56
St James'	60
The Honeybourne Line	64
Race Day Specials	65
Bishops Cleeve, Gotherington, Gretton	66
Winchcombe	70
Hayles Abbey	72
Toddington	73
Cheltenham High Street	75
Cleeve	78
Ashchurch	80
A Few Hours At Ashchurch	84
Evesham Line	89
Tewkesbury Line	90
Tewkesbury	92

ACKNOWLEDGEMENTS

In compiling this book, I have learned a lot from friends and fellow enthusiasts much more knowledgeable than myself, who have given generously of their time and expertise. I would like to thank Peter Witts for reading the main text, for his considerable research over the years into local railway and industrial history, for always knowing where to find source material and for providing much guidance on the whole project. Many other people contributed freely, including Roger Wales, Jim Irwin, Mike Barnsley, David Bick, also various members of the North Gloucestershire Railway Co. Ltd. and their archive material. For quite superb photographic contributions, I must thank, in particular, Bill Potter, John Dagley-Morris and Ben Brooksbank (who also guided me to the fine pictures by E. R. Morten), as well as Robin Stanton, whose views from the signal box, while at work, help to give a different perspective. Finally I am most grateful for all the interest and effort shown towards this book by everyone I approached and I take responsibility for any errors of fact.

BIBLIOGRAPHY
(also see titles mentioned in main text)

R. H. Clark – *An Historical Survey of Selected Great Western Stations, Vol. 3,* Oxford Publishing Co.

J. H. Russell – *The Banbury and Cheltenham Railway 1887-1962,* Oxford Publishing Co.

H. Household – *Gloucestershire Railways in the Twenties,* Alan Sutton

C. Maggs and P. Nicholson – *The Honeybourne Line,* Line One

C. J. Allen – *Titled Trains of Great Britain,* Ian Allan

E. T. MacDermot – *History of the GWR*

J. Gough – *The Midland Railway – A Chronology,* RCHS

R. A. Cooke – *Track Layout Diagrams of the GWR and BR(WR)*

Locos of the GWR, RCTS

G. Hart – *A History of Cheltenham,* Alan Sutton

GWR Magazine

Railway World articles by E. C. B. Thornton in 1963 and 1980

Various working timetables of the Midland Railway, GWR and BR

Various issues of the *Cheltenham Examiner* and *Cheltenham Chronicle*

Above: Midland 2-4-0s had a very long association with the area and this portrait goes back to their early years. Kirtley 2-4-0 No. 82 stands at Lansdown on a down train in the autumn of 1863, with a fascinating variety of early rolling stock. The engine had been constructed at Derby in September 1862, as one of the six 80 Class, with 6' 2" driving wheels, especially to work trains to the 1862 Exhibition in London. After that, No. 82 went to the Birmingham area. As can be seen from other photographs in this book, Lansdown station remained substantially unaltered at platform level throughout the steam era.   *P. Witts Coll*

Middle: Two Midland 2-4-0s stand at the down platform with a local train in the early years of the century. Apart from the engines and stock – note the horsebox behind the second engine – there is some fine lineside furniture; the shunting signal in the foreground, the different loading gauges for the Midland and MSWJ, the signal gantry, water column with lamp aloft and advertisements up on the wall.

J. D. Blyth Coll

Bottom: One of the very last working Midland 2-4-0s, No. 20216, is station pilot at Lansdown in July 1949, not long before it was taken out of service. The engine never carried its allocated BR No. 58022. Based at Gloucester (Barnwood), the loco was such a celebrity by this time that a picture of it appeared in the local newspaper.   *W. Potter*

HISTORICAL SURVEY

GLOUCESTER & CHELTENHAM TRAMROAD

It is appropriate to commence with the Gloucester & Cheltenham Tramroad, of 3'6" gauge, which predated the coming of main line railways in the area. The primary purpose of this concern was the conveyance of stone and other materials from quarries at Leckhampton Hill to the docks at Gloucester. The tramroad, opened in June 1811, was worked by horses, but did experiment, unsuccessfully as it turned out, with steam power. There was apparently a proposal in 1825 to use a flash boiler locomotive and an aborted attempt in 1831 or 1832 to travel from Gloucester with an 0-6-0 locomotive, *Royal William,* built by Neath Abbey Ironworks. A full account of the enterprise can be found in David Bick's excellent book *The Gloucester & Cheltenham Tramroad* (Oakwood Press).

Mention should also be made that it was possible from February 1831, for a short experimental period, to travel from Cheltenham to Gloucester by steam coach on the turnpike road.

According to a local newspaper, it was July 1839 before a steam railway locomotive reached Cheltenham, and, even then, it was drawn by twelve horses through the town to the railway of the Cheltenham and Great Western Union Railway (C&GWU), at the end of the Lansdown Place. The locomotive, engaged by the contractor building the railway between Lansdown Road, Cheltenham and Barnwood Road, Gloucester, was named *The Excavator* and was said to weigh between eleven and twelve tons. But, before long, the first main line railway commenced operation through Cheltenham.

BIRMINGHAM & GLOUCESTER RAILWAY

In 1839 the Birmingham & Gloucester Railway (B&G) started work on building Cheltenham Lansdown station near the Cheltenham and Gloucester turnpike road. Opened for public use from 24 June 1840, there was a service of two passenger trains each way from Cheltenham to Bromsgrove, thence road coach to Birmingham, the whole journey being scheduled to take three and a half hours; the rail connection from Bromsgrove to Camp Hill, Birmingham opened throughout on 17 December 1840. Soon the railway was offering a service of eight trains each way between Cheltenham and Birmingham, with a journey time of less than three hours, and, from 17 August 1841, connections at Curzon Street, Birmingham with the London & Birmingham Railway. Meanwhile, the B&G had started operating from Cheltenham to Gloucester on 4 November 1840, using the railway formation built by the C&GWU on which the B&G had laid its track, as authorised by an Act of 1838.

Trains to Birmingham were faced with the ascent of the infamously steep Lickey incline near Bromsgrove and the B&G ordered locomotives from the USA, which were considered by the railway to be the best available for coping with the gradient involved.

From the outset operations at Cheltenham were hampered by Lansdown's short platforms, forcing many trains to draw up twice – this problem remained for over 120 years, as the platforms were not lengthened until 1965. The station was, and still is, situated on a sharp curve, causing non-stop trains, even today, to have to reduce speed considerably.

At least Cheltenham was spared the even greater operating problems of break of gauge which took place down the line at Gloucester, from July 1844, between the standard 4ft 8 and a half inch gauge Birmingham & Gloucester and the broad 7ft and a half inch gauge of the Bristol and Gloucester Railway and the Great Western Railway (GWR) from London and Swindon.

In early 1845 the Bristol & Gloucester and Birmingham & Gloucester Railways proposed to amalgamate and, in the interim, formed a joint board of management. However, the Midland Railway became involved and both railways were leased to the Midland from July 1845. The full history of those early years is contained in *The Birmingham & Gloucester Railway* by Rev W Awdry (Alan Sutton Publishing) and *The Bristol & Gloucester Railway* by C. Maggs (Oakwood Press).

The route through Cheltenham became the most important cross country line on the Midland Railway, being the main north east – south west route, a role it continues to play in the modern railway network. Given this importance and the number of trains that pass through, Lansdown station seems something of a Cinderella, being a rather modest and unaltered structure for such an important town at which most trains stop. A traveller from the 1840s would have little difficulty in recognising the station as it is in the 1990s; the grand Greek Doric colonnade at the entrance has been demolished, but the two original platforms remain in place. Lesser towns which no longer have any rail services had far grander stations and, indeed, Cheltenham's St James' was a much more impressive station, but this did not save it from closure and demolition. So the legacy of the Birmingham & Gloucester lives on over 150 years later, in the physically restricted and operationally awkward layout at Lansdown.

The exterior of Lansdown station, on the Queen's Road side, showing the fine colonnade which was removed in the 1950s, due to being apparently unsafe. An interesting array of cars, including several taxis, is on display.
Lens of Sutton

ROUTES AROUND ASHCHURCH

Ashchurch station opened on 24 June 1840, as part of the inauguration of the Birmingham & Gloucester Railway between Bromsgrove and Cheltenham on that day. The branch from Ashchurch to Tewkesbury was not far behind, opening on 21 July 1840. The use of locomotives on the branch was forbidden by act of parliament – this was seen as a measure necessary to protect the public, due to the existence of three level crossings in Tewkesbury. Despite the act, a locomotive hauled train was apparently used on the opening day. The station was built next to the High Street, while a proposed extension to the quay for goods traffic caused great public controversy and violent protest, only being finally opened around 1844. Although the act forbidding locomotives was never repealed, all traffic from 18 February 1844, except for the horse-worked night mail, was hauled by locomotives. It is believed, however, that there were further periods of horse working.

A few years later, the Tewkesbury and Malvern Railway Act came into being in 1860, authorising a line from Tewkesbury to Malvern Wells, which opened to traffic on 16 May 1864; a link to Great Malvern station on the Worcester to Hereford line had already opened on 1 July 1862. On the opening to Malvern Wells, the station at Tewkesbury High Street was closed to passengers, as it was now only a branch off the new line, and a station for Tewkesbury was opened on the Malvern line. The new line was worked from the start by the Midland Railway, into which the Tewkesbury and Malvern Railway was vested from 1 July 1877.

Meanwhile the Midland Railway had opened a line from Evesham to Ashchurch, on 1 July 1864 for goods and 1 October 1864 for passengers. At the latter date, the Ashchurch curve also came into use; this went from the Evesham line across the main Birmingham-Bristol line and connected into the line to Tewkesbury. This made it one of the few flat crossings over a main line in the country. Ashchurch now had platforms on three different routes – the main line and the lines to Tewkesbury and Evesham. The main station building was in the vee between the up main platform and the single platform face of the Tewkesbury line. The station even boasted a pub which lasted into BR days. Evesham line trains left from the single face platform on the down main side of the station.

A stationmaster's house and back-to-back houses for other employees were built nearby, as was a large four storey brick-built provender store, which provided fodder for railway horses on the Midland Railway system. Freight and passenger traffic at Ashchurch received a large boost in the early 1940s when a huge army vehicle depot was built beyond the station next to the Evesham line.

Ashchurch was the scene of a fatal accident on a foggy morning early in 1929, when a freight reversing from the up to the down line was hit by a Bristol-Leeds express which had overrun signals. Two passengers and two railwaymen were killed.

How much traffic regularly went over the flat crossing is not known, but it was reduced from two tracks to one by 1927. It was certainly still used in the late 1940s for turning the whole Evesham line train – an engine and three or four coaches.

On the Malvern line, one track beyond Tewkesbury on the double track to Upton had only been used for wagon storage for many years. The entire service from Great Malvern to Upton ceased on and from 1 December 1952, effectively making Ashchurch to Upton a branch. The passenger service was taken off on and from 14 August 1961, remaining steam to the end. A late addition on the branch was a brand new bridge over the M50 motorway near Ripple, which saw very little use. Freight services to Upton continued until 1 July 1963, while those to Tewkesbury ceased on and from 2 November 1964.

The flat crossing was officially taken out of use in May 1957 and the track lifted immediately. Over on the Evesham side, passenger and freight continued until the former stopped on and from 17 June 1963 and the latter shortly afterwards on and from 1 July 1963. But passenger trains had run only between Ashchurch and Evesham since 1 October 1962, as the track beyond to Redditch was so poor that buses were substituted on that section.

In the meantime stations on the main line around Ashchurch were also suffering closures – to the south, Cleeve had closed to passengers as long ago as February 1950, the ones to the north such as Bredon and Defford survived until 4 January 1965. Ashchurch itself became an unstaffed halt, but saw out the end of steam on BR and finally closed on and from 15 November 1971, only local trains having stopped there for some years. The army camp continued to provide freight traffic into the early 1990s, until the withdrawal of BR's Speedlink service, usually being handled by a pick-up freight from Gloucester, along with the occasional special train. Nowadays there is talk of reopening a station here, so Ashchurch (for Tewkesbury) may yet reappear on the railway map.

Neither was steam quite dead at Ashchurch, as the Dowty Railway Preservation Society had become established on the old provender store sidings, with steam locomotives being based there from 1963. During the steam ban era on BR in the late 1960s, engines used to leave here in steam regardless for open day displays at Tyseley in Birmingham and at Bristol Bath Road. On the Ashchurch site, regular steam days were held for many years, providing passing travellers on the main line with a reminder of the steam era, which, for Ashchurch, stretched back to 1840.

Caprotti 'Black 5' No. 44744 heads a down express towards the flat crossing on 9 October 1955. By this time, the crossing only had one track, the second having been removed in the late 1920s. *E. R. Morten*

Here is part of the impressive exterior of St James' station, opened in 1894, with the canopy over the entrance road and the double gates to the goods shed. The booking hall, waiting rooms and station offices were all in the main building.

E. Wilmshurst

Residents of Cheltenham had for some time wanted a railway to London and a meeting on 13 October 1835 called for a railway to Swindon to join up with the Great Western Railway line proposed from Bristol to London. The GWR supported the move, but there was a parliamentary battle with the London and Birmingham Railway who backed a scheme for a line from Tring in Hertfordshire to Cheltenham; nevertheless the Cheltenham & Great Western Union Act came into force in 1836, authorising a broad gauge line to Swindon via Gloucester, Stonehouse, Stroud, Chalford and Kemble, with a branch from the latter place to Cirencester.

The C&GWU agreed with the Birmingham & Gloucester Railway to construct a joint line (making it the first such railway in the country) between Cheltenham and Gloucester, despite the C&GWU being broad gauge and the B&G standard gauge. The two companies also agreed to jointly purchase the Gloucester & Cheltenham Tramroad (which was worked until 1859 by their successors, the GWR and Midland Railway).

After some initial activity (see page 5), nothing much happened at the Cheltenham end of the C&GWU, due to various disputes and financial difficulties and the company was taken over by the GWR on 1 July 1843. These two companies were amalgamated by the Great Western Act of 1844, which also authorised the broad gauge extension from Lansdown Road to St James'. Construction began in 1844, but was suspended due to the possibility of a line being built from Cheltenham to Shipton-under-Wychwood on the Oxford, Worcester and Wolverhampton Railway, which would have siphoned off potential traffic.

The broad gauge finally opened from Gloucester to the dead-end station at St James' Square, Cheltenham on 23 October 1847 (the station was named Cheltenham (St James) from 1908 and Cheltenham Spa (St James) from 1 February 1925).

Between Tramway Junction, Gloucester and Lansdown Junction, Cheltenham was mixed gauge track, the first significant meeting in the country of the rival gauges. Trains were limited to eight miles an hour across Lansdown Junction, where the former Birmingham & Gloucester – now Midland Railway – standard gauge line split off to Lansdown station and Birmingham. The GWR was the legal owner of the joint line from 1845, but only as trustee for the Midland over the half nearer Gloucester. The legal arrangement changed in 1867 when this half was conveyed to the Midland. Each company had free use of the other's half and each kept its own half in repair. The halfway post was just south of Churchdown station.

Trains from Cheltenham to Swindon ran via the Gloucester avoiding line until 1851, stopping at the so-called T station from where a shuttle service operated the short distance into Gloucester. With a connection at Swindon, some fast journey times were possible between Cheltenham and London Paddington in those early years – the 9.50am from the capital ran the 120 miles in two hours and forty-seven minutes, changing trains at Swindon, and three other trains gave a three hour service.

The complications of mixed gauge between Cheltenham and Gloucester were nothing compared with the chaos at the latter, traffic from Bristol, South Wales and the Swindon line heading north on the Midland Railway arrived on the broad gauge and left on the standard gauge, with a terrible confusion of goods and passengers – so much so that questions were asked in parliament and cartoonists had a field day in the press depicting the scenes of confusion. Eventually, of course, all broad gauge lines were converted to standard gauge, the section from Gloucester to St James' being completed in May 1872.

St James' was extensively enlarged in the 1890s to accommodate more and longer passenger trains, while an imposing new canopy at St James' Square enabled passengers to transfer to and from their horse-drawn road carriages under cover. A new goods shed was also erected and the goods yard was expanded to accommodate 475 wagons. The new station opened on 9 September 1894, about 500 feet from the old one.

When the line to Honeybourne was constructed in the early years of this century, St James', despite being quite an imposing station, was really relegated to being on a short spur off the main GWR route between Birmingham and Bristol. It was used mainly by local services to Gloucester and beyond, the auto trains to Honeybourne and the Kingham line service. The latter's potential was never greatly exploited by the GWR – it provided a much shorter route to London than via Gloucester, Kemble and Swindon. The only express departures were the through trains to London Paddington, four in number in later steam days, including The Cheltenham Spa Express, which found great fame in the 1920s, when it was popularly known as the Cheltenham Flyer.

In November 1958, it became the terminus for the remnants of the old Midland & South Western Junction Railway (MSWJ) service to Southampton, until this expired in September 1961. The Honeybourne line auto trains had already ceased in March 1960 and the Kingham line succumbed to closure in October 1962. The number of trains starting and terminating at St James' steadily dwindled as other services, such as to Hereford, ceased; diesels had completely taken over the Paddington trains from the end of October 1964 and diesel multiple units worked most of the remaining stopping trains, so that by the late autumn of 1965, usually just one train from Gloucester was steam. With lengthening of the platforms at Lansdown station, Paddington trains could start from there and the inevitable happened on 1 January 1966, when the last passenger train ran into St James', with the station

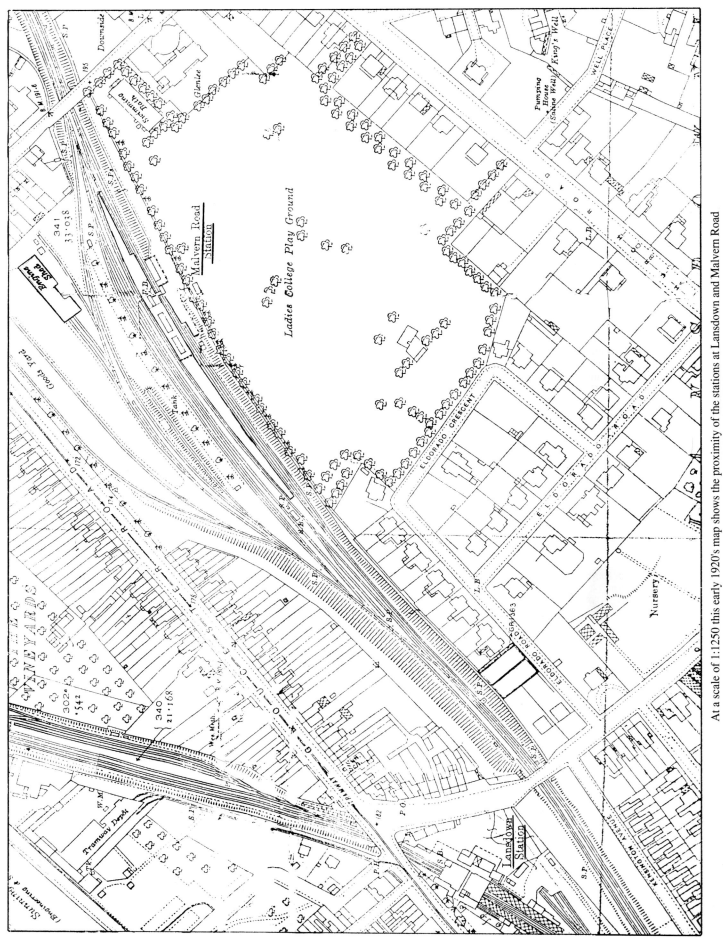

At a scale of 1:1250 this early 1920's map shows the proximity of the stations at Lansdown and Malvern Road

8

closing on and from 3 January for passengers and on 31 October 1966 for goods. Despite a spirited local campaign to save St James' – whose location close to the town centre and the country bus station made it much more convenient for many passengers than Lansdown which is on the outskirts of the town – it was eventually demolished and the site then lay derelict for many years, a victim of planning blight.

BANBURY & CHELTENHAM DIRECT RAILWAY

On 1 June 1881, trains started running from the GWR's terminus at St James' Square to Chipping Norton Junction (renamed Kingham in 1909) via Andoversford, Bourton-on-the-Water and Stow-on-the-Wold (the line from Bourton to Chipping Norton Junction had been running since 1862). At Chipping Norton Junction, connection was made with the Worcester-Oxford line and thus to London, also with the line to Chipping Norton and Banbury.

The new section to Bourton, starting from Lansdown Junction, was 16 miles 50 chains and included a fine 12 arch brick viaduct at Dowdeswell and a 384 yard long tunnel at Sandywell Park near Andoversford, as well as grades of 1 in 60 in parts. The railway was formally purchased in 1897 by the GWR, who worked the line from the beginning.

The line from Cheltenham was the fruition of various attempts over a period of some years to run a railway to Oxford. Proposed, but not built, was a route to Oxford via Andoversford, Northleach, Burford and Witney and another via Shipton-under-Wychwood on the Worcester-Oxford line. Also mooted was the East Gloucestershire Railway, a line from Cheltenham to Faringdon via Fairford and on, with a line that actually was built, through Witney to Oxford.

Envisaged as a through route of some importance, it was really not much more than a glorified branch line. It was 1906 before trains were able to run directly from Cheltenham to Banbury, thanks to construction of a bridge over the Worcester-Oxford line at Kingham, enabling through trains to avoid reversal at the latter place. Also in 1906 the Hatherley loop near Cheltenham, from Gloucester Loop Junction to Hatherley Junction – just under half a mile – was laid and a long distance express train, with dining car, at last ran over the line, en route from Newcastle-upon-Tyne to South Wales. As it took the Hatherley loop towards Gloucester, avoiding the main Cheltenham

stations, the train stopped for passengers on the outskirts at Leckhampton station, which was consequently renamed Cheltenham South and Leckhampton. The express ran over the route each way on weekdays until the start of World War 2; after the war, the train was diverted away from the line.

From August 1891, the single track from Lansdown Junction to Andoversford Junction was shared by trains of the Midland & South Western Junction Railway and was doubled from 28 September 1902, remaining so until closure of the line. The section from Andoversford Junction to Kingham West signal box, outside Kingham station, was always single line.

An interesting development in 1922 was the building of a standard gauge railway from Charlton Kings station up Leckhampton Hill via Daisy Bank Road, Southfield Farm and Sandy Lane to the quarries and lime kilns there. Caffin & Co, the contractors who built the line, brought in various equipment, including a Manning Wardle 0-6-0ST, No. 1432 of 1899, named *Fashoda*, and a narrow gauge petrol Motor Rail loco, to help with the works. The new line was about one and a quarter miles long, two-thirds of a mile being in the form of a cable worked incline. The operators, Leckhampton Quarries Co Ltd, acquired their own 0-4-0ST, Peckett No. 906 of 1902, named *Lightmoor*, which worked wagons from the foot of the incline to the exchange sidings at Charlton Kings station. This company did not last long and receivers were appointed in October 1925, the quarry being finally closed in November 1926, with the plant, engine and track being auctioned in August 1927. A full account of the enterprise is contained in *Old Leckhampton* (Runpast Publishing, 1993).

The line, and all stations, from Lansdown Junction to, but excluding, Bourton-on-the-Water closed to all traffic on and from 15 October 1962 (the section from Bourton-on-the-Water to Kingham lost its passenger service at the same time, but remained open for freight until total closure on and from 7 September 1964).

Track lifting both on the Kingham line and the old MSWJ took some time. It was 10 February 1965 before the track was lifted as far back as the old Gloucester Loop Junction (removed in the 1950s), with 2-6-2T No. 4100 in charge on the dismantling train and it was 16 May 1965 before the connection at Lansdown Junction was severed. At this time, Leckhampton station was being demolished.

Gloucester Loop Junction and signal box is shown here, with the line to Lansdown Junction on the right. The line to the left is the short spur to Hatherley Junction, opened in early 1906, enabling trains to bypass Cheltenham and head directly towards Gloucester. It was little used after World War 2, having no regular traffic in the latter years of its existence and was officially closed on 28 August 1956. *M. P. Barnsley Coll*

MIDLAND & SOUTH WESTERN JUNCTION RAILWAY

The Midland & South Western Junction Railway was an independent line which came to form a useful route from the Midlands and North to the important port of Southampton. The company was formed in 1884 by the amalgamation of the Swindon, Marlborough & Andover and Swindon & Cheltenham Extension Railway Companies. Using its own line from Andoversford Junction to Andover Junction and running powers over the Midland, Great Western and London & South Western

Railways (LSWR), it ran trains from Cheltenham through Andoversford, Cirencester, Swindon, Marlborough, Ludgershall and Andover to Southampton, including carriages from the North of England. The line from Cirencester Watermoor, where the railway's workshops were sited, to Andoversford was 14 miles with heavy grades through the beautiful Cotswold countryside. It was expensive to construct, with a good deal of rock cutting and a tunnel at Chedworth, near where the summit of the line had a ruling grade of 1 in 75.

The MSWJ was actually in the hands of the receivers when it commenced regular passenger services on 1 August 1891 from Cheltenham Lansdown station to Andover Junction and on over the LSWR to Southampton. Connection to the Midland Railway at Cheltenham proved to be its salvation, as there was such an increase in traffic that the MSWJ was able to discharge the receivers in 1897.

The MSWJ enjoyed good relations with the much larger Midland, who saw the line as a vital link for its traffic to gain access to Southampton Docks. Apart from allowing MSWJ trains into Lansdown station, the Midland also helped financially with the establishment in the 1890s of a goods yard and locomotive shed at Cheltenham High Street, near the gasworks, and carriage sidings and a turntable at the Vineyards just north of Lansdown station. The railway had a distinctive and attractive roster of locomotives, which provided an interesting contrast in Cheltenham with the engines of the Midland and Great Western.

One problem encountered at the Cheltenham end of the route was having to use the single Great Western line from Lansdown Junction to Andoversford Junction, leading to delays and frustration, as, of course, the GWR always gave priority to its own trains. Thus the MSWJ formulated various plans to bypass this problem. These included building a line direct from Andoversford to the Midland at Ashchurch and the Andoversford & Stratford-upon-Avon Railway scheme of 1898. However, these proposals were abandoned when the GWR agreed to double the line from Andoversford Junction to Lansdown Junction. Even then, the GWR did not allow the MSWJ to stop at the former's station at Andoversford Junction until 1 October 1904 – so the MSWJ had its own station at Andoversford & Dowdeswell. Also the MSWJ converted its line between Andoversford Junction and Cirencester from single to double track between 1900 and 1902.

It was an extremely busy railway during both world wars, with traffic, not just for Southampton, but also for the important military installations on Salisbury Plain.

The MSWJ was taken over by the GWR at the grouping of the railways in 1923 and, apart from wartime, suffered a steady decline. For example, the route from Andoversford Junction to Cirencester was reduced to a single line in July 1928. The final blow came when the connection at Lansdown Junction from Lansdown station was removed and passenger trains for Southampton had to start instead at Cheltenham St James' from 3 November 1958. This effectively ended its status as a through route from the Midlands and North of England to Southampton.

The last regular passenger train was the 1.52pm Cheltenham St James' to Southampton on Saturday 9 September 1961 hauled by Southern Region 2-6-0 No. 31791 with the usual complement of three coaches. In the area covered by this book, the line closed to all traffic on and from 11 September 1961 (except that Andoversford & Dowdeswell remained open for goods traffic until the closure on 15 October 1962 of the Kingham line through Andoversford).

The full history of the MSWJ, affectionately known as the 'Tiddley Dyke', is contained in the three volume *Midland & South Western Junction Railway* (Wild Swan Publications).

A World War 1 shot looking north from Lansdown bridge shows the Honeybourne line junction layout on the routes to Lansdown station, left, and Malvern Road station, right, also the junction signal box opened in May 1914 and closed on the widening in 1942. The train is an MSWJ local headed by one of their 0-6-0s. After passing under Lansdown bridge, the train will head off up the Andoversford line.
A. B. MacLeod Coll/N.R.M. York

The upheaval caused by the construction of the Honeybourne line is shown well in this print taken at St George's Road, Cheltenham. Several contractors wagons in the photo are presumably drawn by the horse pictured.
M. P. Barnsley Coll

GREAT WESTERN RAILWAY – CHELTENHAM to HONEYBOURNE

The Honeybourne line was a comparative latecomer onto the main railway network. As the Great Western Railway magazine put it in 1904, in an article written by James C. Inglis, the general manager of the GWR:

'Like all important new routes it had been talked of for years as a line the Great Western Company ought to make, but its great cost must be considered the main reason why its construction was not embarked upon earlier . . . a combination of circumstances added reasons . . . for its being undertaken. These were the increasingly rapid development of fruit culture, and also indications that, with better railway facilities, the growing of vegetables on a large scale would become commercially possible. A further reason was the great increase in the Company's North and South traffic over their existing lines . . .'

However, after these worthy sentiments, the postscript added possibly the main reason the GWR had finally decided to act:

'and lastly, a proposal to cut off this rich district, situated between Great Western Railway main lines, from its natural and efficient development by the GWR.'

This last was probably a reference to the threat by the Midland & South Western Junction Railway to build a line from Andoversford to Stratford-upon-Avon (see the MSWJ summary). While the MSWJ lacked the resources to construct the line, its friends on the Midland Railway would probably have been interested in supporting such a venture, in order to tap the traffic potential of the area.

The total length of the line to be constructed was quoted at about twenty-one and a half miles, with building starting at the Honeybourne end; it connected with, and crossed, the Oxford-Worcester line. The line was constructed throughout as double track and opened for traffic as follows:

Honeybourne to Broadway		1 August 1904
Broadway to Toddington	(goods)	1 August 1904
	(passenger)	1 December 1904
Toddington to Winchcombe		1 February 1905
Winchcombe to Bishops Cleeve		2 June 1906
Bishops Cleeve to Cheltenham (Malvern Road Junction)		1 August 1906
Cheltenham Malvern Road station		30 March 1908

The line was only used as a through route between Birmingham and the West of England and South Wales from 1 July 1908, following the doubling of the line from Stratford-on-Avon to Honeybourne.

Heavy engineering works were required in some parts; between Broadway and Winchcombe, for example, 637,800 cubic yards of earth was excavated. The most imposing structure on this section was, and is, Toddington viaduct, 50 feet high with fifteen 36 feet spans. The tunnel outside Winchcombe is 693 yards long and the one near Cheltenham racecourse, at Hunting Butts, is 97 yards long. A fair amount of property had to be demolished in the St Paul's area of Cheltenham to make way for the railway and extensive retaining walls had to be constructed where the line passed through on embankments.

In the early days, before the line opened to Cheltenham, a steam rail motor service operated from Honeybourne to Winchcombe, with a connecting road motor car service to Cheltenham. The steam rail motors were, in later years, replaced by auto trains, an 0-4-2 tank locomotive pushing or pulling one or more trailers. This service lasted until 5 March 1960, at which time all the intermediate stations and halts between Cheltenham (Malvern Road) and Honeybourne, except Cheltenham Race Course which stayed open, and Gotherington Halt which shut down on and from 13 June 1955, closed to passenger traffic.

The daily through passenger trains (see Traffic Flows section) were diverted onto the ex-Midland Railway route via Ashchurch from 10 September 1962, including the *Cornishman*, now dieselised, another blow for the route, although seasonal trains from the Midlands to the West of England and South Wales continued to use the line until 1966, the last steam-hauled passenger train being on 4 September 1965. Steam freight and parcels trains still worked over the route in 1965 and into 1966, including trains diverted from the Ashchurch main line.

Malvern Road station closed down on and from 3 January 1966 and Lansdown Junction to Stratford-upon-Avon was closed to regular passenger traffic from 25 March 1968, by then being reduced to the daily passage of a single car diesel unit between Leamington Spa and Gloucester. Specials and race trains still ran from time to time. Stations such as Bishops Cleeve and Winchcombe had been demolished by the summer of 1965.

Freight used the route long after the demise of steam – though three preserved steam locos traversed the line in August 1975, returning from 150th anniversary celebrations in North East England – until August 1976 when a train derailed at Winchcombe, effectively ending commercial use on the section covered by this book.

Then the preservationists arrived, but that is another story . . .

WIDENING BETWEEN CHELTENHAM AND GLOUCESTER

The two track railway between Cheltenham Lansdown Junction and Gloucester Engine Shed Junction had always been very busy, being on the most important cross-country route for the Midland Railway and with heavy traffic for the GWR. The demands of World War 2 made a necessity of widening the route from two to four tracks, a large undertaking in view of the scarcity of resources, but it was obviously deemed to be an essential wartime measure. The work was shared jointly by the GWR and London Midland & Scottish Railway (LMS), but financed by the Ministry of Supply.

Heavy work was required, including the complete remodelling of Lansdown Junction and rebuilding of bridges at Lansdown, Hatherley, Badgeworth and Churchdown, as well as new signal boxes at all these places, together with improvement and replacement of all the associated signalling and earthworks. The new lines and equipment were phased in during 1942, starting from the Gloucester end, between Engine Shed Junction and Elm Bridge on 3 May; on 5 and 12 July between Elm Bridge and Churchdown; on 9 August between Churchdown and Hatherley Junction; and on 23 August between Hatherley Junction and Lansdown Junction. The new signal boxes at Hatherley Junction and Lansdown Junction were brought into use between 26 and 31 July. As for signalling, the GWR erected lower quadrants from Lansdown Junction to the halfway point just south of Churchdown station and the LMS provided its upper quadrants from there to Gloucester.

Until the widening, GWR trains had been designated DOWN between Gloucester and Cheltenham, but LMS trains were designated UP in this direction and vice-versa from Cheltenham to Gloucester. This anomaly disappeared and all trains took on the LMS designation.

Going north, the four tracks were designated: up main; up relief; down main; down relief. While the LMS trains mostly used the up relief towards Birmingham, they used the down main towards Gloucester. Similarly, the GWR used the up main and down relief – this meant that GWR up trains crossed over down LMS trains at Lansdown Junction, but otherwise conflicting movements were kept to a minimum.

A large mound of earth was excavated from the cutting at the Reddings, near Hatherley, and dumped on higher ground near the railway, where it remained for many years, until removed to make way for houses. At Cloddymore, the foot crossing was replaced by a footbridge.

As traffic on the railways declined in the 1960s and more modern signalling systems came into use, the need for four tracks receded and the two relief lines from Lansdown Junction to Churchdown were taken out of use at the beginning of September 1966, just around the time a BR steam locomotive on a BR commercial train last put in an appearance on the route. The 'new' signal box at the erstwhile Hatherley Junction closed on 20 November 1966 and the box and relief lines from Churchdown towards Gloucester suffered a similar fate in early 1967. The relief lines were eventually pulled up and the two remaining tracks realigned. With the introduction of power signalling in the area in 1969, controlled from Gloucester, Lansdown Junction signal box then operated just the connection to the Honeybourne line, for which it was specially opened when trains were due on that route. Following official closure between Cheltenham and Honeybourne in October 1977, the remaining parts of the junction, except for a set of facing points into a down refuge loop, were removed and the box was closed from 12 November 1977.

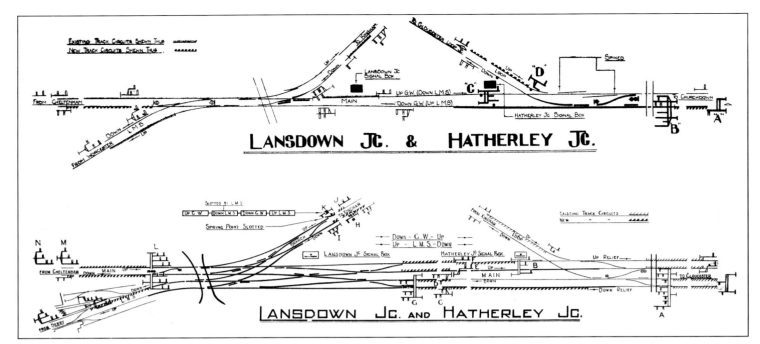

Track and signalling, before and after the widening, between Lansdown Junction and Hatherley Junction, Cheltenham – July 1942 (top), August 1942 (bottom) from official GWR working notices.

TRAFFIC FLOWS

As already stated, the line through Cheltenham was the most important cross-country route on the Midland Railway's map, connecting Bristol and Birmingham and thus just about anywhere in the country. Freight and passenger traffic flowed from North West and North East to South West England and South Wales and vice-versa. The ocean going port of Southampton could be reached by way of the MSWJ and the South of England via the Somerset & Dorset Joint Railway at Bath. Summer holiday traffic was particularly heavy for the West of England from the large industrial conurbations in the Midlands and North of England. All contributed to a constant stream of trains through Lansdown station day and night. At Lansdown Junction converged the trains of the GWR from Wolverhampton, Birmingham, Banbury, Gloucester, South Wales, Swindon and Bristol, making the signal box there very busy indeed. Even in the 1950s, it was possible to observe between 150 and 200 trains on a summer Saturday in a 12 hour period. It was common during the peak for every signalling block on all four lines between Cheltenham and Gloucester to be occupied by trains, with plenty more in front of, and behind, them.

On the freight side, coal came down from the Midlands mines and up from the South Wales pits; iron ore travelled from the Oxfordshire fields and further afield to the South Wales steelworks and finished steel products went in both directions; trains of manufactured goods such as cars from Austins at Longbridge came through, while oil flowed from the refineries at Fawley, near Southampton, to the terminal at Bromford Bridge, north of Birmingham; the beer train from the breweries of Burton went down to Bristol; bananas came up from Avonmouth docks, while fruit grown in the Vale of Evesham was distributed to all corners. Parcels and newspaper trains added to the traffic, while livestock and the seasonal racing pigeon specials from the north increased the variety. Trains of military equipment headed for various strategic destinations, while the railways' own requirements added rail and ballast trains and permanent way works trains, as well as van trains of locomotive and rolling stock parts. Well into the 1950s, freights still left Cheltenham High Street goods yard bound for the MSWJ line and Southampton. Local traffic hauled in pick-up and transfer freights called at wayside stations and yards to drop off fertiliser, coal, animal feed and agricultural implements. Empty stock trips and light engine movements contributed to the busy scene.

The Midland line through Cheltenham was always busy with long-distance passenger services, whilst the GWR route from Honeybourne only really came alive during the summer months. However the GWR did cause the MR some problems in the early years of the Honeybourne

line, when many passengers transferred their loyalties to the GWR between Bristol and Birmingham, forcing the Midland, which had enjoyed a monopoly between those two cities for so many years, to speed up its services. On the Midland, the main flow of daily through trains came down from Newcastle-upon-Tyne, York, Bradford, Leeds, Sheffield and Nottingham to Bristol and Cardiff and beyond. The main train from the north west came from Manchester and travelled over the Somerset & Dorset Railway to Bournemouth. On the GWR Honeybourne line, there were four expresses each way by 1914 and five by 1922, while in later years there were just two or three trains from Birmingham to South Wales and the Wolverhampton to Penzance passenger. The GWR was rather progressive on this line when it introduced express diesel railcars pre-war on the South Wales run, although due to having limited capacity, even when running in multiple unit form, they were often replaced by steam-hauled trains. In the summer months, the Honeybourne line was busier, with holiday trains from Wolverhampton and Birmingham to destinations in the West Country and South Wales.

There was a busy service of local and stopping passenger train departures from Cheltenham (St James') to Gloucester Central, thence various destinations such as Swindon, Cardiff, Hereford and Ledbury. Cheltenham (Lansdown) to Gloucester (Eastgate) was served by Birmingham (New Street) and Worcester (Shrub Hill) to Gloucester and Bristol all stations services, as well as the long distance expresses.

Then there were the through expresses from St James' to London Paddington – in 1960-61 there were four on weekdays, leaving at 7.5am, 8am, 11.45am and 4pm. Until 5 March 1960, auto trains also left St James' for the Honeybourne line, stopping at most stations and halts – some trains went beyond Honeybourne, to Evesham, while others stopped short at Broadway. Trains for Kingham left St James' over the years between four and six times every weekday. This route provided a viable alternative for travellers to London, as, with a good connection at Kingham on trains from Worcester, the travel time was very comparable with the longer route via Gloucester, Kemble and Swindon taken by the through Cheltenham-Paddington trains. Indeed, in pre-grouping days, even the MSWJ provided a competitive alternative to London (Waterloo) by changing at Andover Junction, which was faster – at 3 hours 19 minutes – than some of the GWR services through Swindon.

In its heyday, before World War 1, the MSWJ passenger service of seven daily trains over the route included the *North Express* and *South Express*, tightly timed and worked over the difficult 69 miles between

12

Andover and Cheltenham, and conveying through London & North Western Railway corridor coaches between Southampton and Liverpool or Manchester. With access to Southampton and the passenger ships there, Lansdown station was able to boast, on the station nameboard, 'change here for Paris'. After the grouping, and takeover by the GWR, the MSWJ route was gradually run down – by the mid-1950s there were just three daily passenger trains each way between Cheltenham and Andover. This was reduced to one south and two north even before the line was severed at Lansdown Junction in November 1958, after which only one passenger train each way survived to trundle in and out of St James' and through freight virtually ceased.

The rather leisurely service from Newcastle-upon-Tyne to South Wales via Hatherley loop has already been mentioned in the Banbury and Cheltenham Direct Railway section. This was unofficially named the *Ports-to-Ports Express* and coaching stock was provided by the London & North Eastern Railway (LNER) and GWR on alternate days.

Other named expresses travelled through Cheltenham over the years. In 1927 a Bradford to Bristol express was named the *Devonian* by the Midland Railway – in fact only three coaches of this train made it into Devon, being attached to a GWR train at Bristol for the trip to Paignton. The train was accelerated greatly in 1937 and became very fast on the Birmingham-Bristol section. After descending the Lickey incline, the service was timed at a mile a minute from Bromsgrove to Cheltenham, which also applied to the northbound *Devonian*. In the summer months, the whole train ran through to Kingswear, complete with restaurant cars. The through service did not run in wartime, but commenced again in 1946, albeit on slower timings. It survived into the diesel era.

The *Pines Express* came into being also in 1927, running from Manchester (with through coaches from Liverpool) to Bournemouth via Birmingham, Cheltenham and Bath, on the Somerset & Dorset Joint Railway; a through coach to Southampton was detached at Cheltenham and worked over the MSWJ route, the same happening in the northbound direction. Again this service had a mile a minute schedule between Cheltenham and Bromsgrove from 1937. The train disappeared in wartime and when it restarted in October 1946, there was no longer a coach for Southampton.

The most famous train with which Cheltenham is connected is the *Cheltenham Flyer* – known throughout the world in its heyday – although this was never an official name, officialdom had christened it the somewhat duller *Cheltenham Spa Express*. The train started after World War 1 as an afternoon service from Cheltenham to Paddington, but it was in 1923 that it started to hit the headlines. The GWR chose it to try and claim the speed record on British railways; it was timed to cover the easily graded route from Swindon to Paddington in 75 minutes for the 77.3 miles, giving a start-to-stop average of 61.8 miles an hour. This made it slightly faster than the previous record holder, the LNER. In July 1929 the train covered the distance in 70 minutes, making the average 66.2 miles an hour, the fastest regular train in the world. The Canadians snatched the record later, so the train was speeded up again, to 67 minutes – an average of 69.2 miles an hour, in September 1931. A year later, the figures were 65 minutes and 71.4 miles an hour, and the *Cheltenham Flyer* again held the world record. The fastest ever recorded run was on 6 June 1932 when engine No. 5006 *Tregenna Castle*, with six coaches, ran the 77.3 miles at an average of 81.7 miles an hour. However, it must be said that all the excitement was confined to the Swindon-Paddington section – progress from St James' to Swindon was very average, taking 71 minutes for the 44.25 miles, due to the severe nature of the grades in the Stroud valley and stops at Malvern Road, Gloucester Central, where the train also reversed, Stroud and Kemble. The *Cheltenham Spa Express* did not reappear after the war until 11 June 1956, and only as a very ordinary service throughout, leaving St James' at 8am. On the day it restarted, the local newspaper printed a picture of a glamorous 'Castle' on the train, but, in truth, the haulage from Cheltenham to Gloucester was taken by a more prosaic 2-6-2T, albeit carrying the *Cheltenham Spa Express* headboard, with the 'Castle' going forward to Paddington.

The other regular named express in the area covered by this book was the *Cornishman,* used from the summer of 1952 for the Wolverhampton to Penzance daily train, via Stratford-upon-Avon, Cheltenham Spa (Malvern Road), Gloucester (Eastgate) and Bristol. The *Cornishman* was one of the few express passenger trains on the Honeybourne line and, at holiday times, ran in two or more parts. It was

The Cornishman

WEEKDAYS

		a.m.				a.m.
WOLVERHAMPTON (Low Level)	... dep.	9A 0	PENZANCE	... dep.		10A10
Bilston Central ...	... ,,	9A 6	St. Erth	... ,,		10A22
Wednesbury Central ...	... ,,	9A12	Gwinear Road ...	... ,,		10A35
West Bromwich ...	... ,,	9A20	Camborne	... ,,		10A43
Birmingham (Snow Hill) ...	... ,,	9A40	Redruth	... ,,		10A52
Stratford-upon-Avon ...	... ,,	10 19	Truro	... ,,		11A12
Cheltenham Spa (Malvern Road)	... ,,	11 2	St. Austell	... ,,		11 37
Gloucester Eastgate ...	... ,,	11 20	Par	... ,,		11 46
		p.m.				p.m.
Bristol (Temple Meads)	... arr.	12 15	Bodmin Road... ...	... ,,		12 1
Taunton	... ,,	1 15	Liskeard	... ,,		12 20
Exeter (St. David's) ...	... ,,	1 58	Plymouth	... ,,		1 0
Dawlish	... ,,	2 33	Kingswear	... ,,		12A15
Teignmouth	... ,,	2 41	Churston (for Brixham) ...	... ,,		12A30
Newton Abbot ...	... ,,	2 51	Goodrington Sands Halt ...	... ,,		12B40
Torre	... ,,	3 8	Paignton	... ,,		12A55
Torquay	... ,,	3 11	Torquay	... ,,		1A 2
Paignton	... ,,	3 21	Torre	... ,,		1 7
Goodrington Sands Halt ...	... ,,	3B24	Kingskerswell	... ,,		1 15
Churston (for Brixham) ...	... ,,	3 30	Newton Abbot ...	... ,,		1 23
Kingswear	... ,,	3 41	Teignmouth	... ,,		1 34
Plymouth	... ,,	3 20	Dawlish	... ,,		1 42
Liskeard	... ,,	3 59	Exeter (St. David's) ...	... ,,		2 24
Bodmin Road... ...	... ,,	4 15	Taunton	... ,,		3 5
Par	... ,,	4 28	Bristol (Temple Meads) ...	... ,,		4 8
St. Austell	... ,,	4 39	Gloucester Eastgate ...	... arr.		5 3
Truro	... ,,	5 3	Cheltenham Spa (Malvern Rd.)	... ,,		5 21
Redruth	... ,,	5 29	Stratford-upon-Avon ...	... ,,		6 5
Carn Brea	... ,,	5 34	Birmingham (Snow Hill) ...	... ,,		6 49
Camborne	... ,,	5 40	West Bromwich	... ,,		7 4
Hayle	... ,,	5 50	Wednesbury Central ...	... ,,		7 12
St. Erth	... ,,	5 57	Bilston Central	... ,,		7 18
Penzance	... ,,	6 10	Wolverhampton (Low Level)	... ,,		7 25

A—Seats can be reserved in advance on payment of a fee of 2s. 0d. per seat.

B—Commences 4th May, 1959.

RESTAURANT CAR SERVICE

Cheltenham Spa Express

WEEKDAYS

		p.m.				a.m.
London (Paddington)	... dep.	4A55	Cheltenham Spa (St. James')	dep.		8A 0
Kemble	... arr.	6 33	Cheltenham Spa (Malvern Road)	... ,,		8A 2
Stroud... ...	... ,,	6 54	Gloucester Central ...	... ,,		8A19
Gloucester Central ...	... ,,	7 12	Stonehouse (Burdett Road)...	,,		8A33
Cheltenham Spa (Malvern Road)	... ,,	7 33	Stroud... ...	... ,,		8A41
Cheltenham Spa (St. James')	... ,,	7 35	Kemble	... ,,		9A 4
			London (Paddington)	... arr.		10 35

A—Seats can be reserved in advance on payment of a fee of 2s. 0d. per seat.

RESTAURANT CAR SERVICE

Famous Named Trains, 15.9.58 to 14.6.59

the first official use of the *Cornishman* name, although it had been used unofficially back in broad gauge days on a train from Paddington to Penzance, which achieved immortal fame as being the last broad gauge express to leave Paddington for stations in Cornwall on 20 May 1892.

Ashchurch was the junction for passenger services on the line to Great Malvern via Tewkesbury, Upton-on-Severn and Malvern Wells, and on the line to Barnt Green via Evesham, Alcester and Redditch. A September 1867 timetable showed four daily trains from Great Malvern, with ten trains on the short journey to and from Tewkesbury, and four trains on the line from Evesham. By September 1960, trains from Ashchurch to Upton-on-Severn totalled just one a day (two in the opposite direction), with an extra one on Saturdays; of course, there were no trains beyond Upton by this time. Additionally there were four shuttles to and from Tewkesbury. On the other line, there were three (four on Saturdays) trains to Redditch, one of which went through to Birmingham (New Street). In the opposite direction, two came through from Birmingham, with one (two on Saturdays) from Redditch. There were no Sunday trains from Ashchurch on either line.

There were sometimes special workings – excursions to Tewkesbury, and in wartime, special ambulance trains to the hospitals and recuperation centres in the Malverns. The Ashchurch to Evesham line was used as a diversionary route when there were problems on the Birmingham-Bristol main line or on the Honeybourne line , although more for freight than passenger.

The line to Evesham was well used by through freight, mainly trains to and from South Wales. Goods trains from Yarnton, near Oxford, worked through Honeybourne to Evesham on the line to Worcester, then diverted onto the Midland line to Ashchurch. Iron ore wagons were gathered at Woodford Halse, on the erstwhile Great Central Railway, for their journey to South Wales steelworks, via the former Stratford-upon-Avon and Midland Junction Railway through Fenny Compton, Stratford and Bidford-on-Avon to Broom Junction, where they connected into the Alcester and Ashchurch line. This traffic was diverted to the Cheltenham-Honeybourne route in 1960. Until September 1960, there was a Mondays-excepted freight from Ashchurch to Washwood Heath via Evesham and Redditch, although coming from the north it only ran as far as Evesham, with the engine running light to Tewkesbury shed for servicing. Additionally, a Tewkesbury based engine ran a pick-up goods between Ashchurch and Evesham, as well as a return trip to Cleeve. A Gloucester (Barnwood Sidings) to Bromsgrove freight also spent time at Ashchurch to shunt traffic for the army camp. The large military depot at Ashchurch had its own diesel shunters which worked out past the station and into the exchange sidings alongside the main line.

Passenger trains at Andoversford Junction were those on the Banbury and Cheltenham line and on the MSWJ, so far as is known no regular passenger trains started or terminated here in the normal course of events. The junction saw many ambulance trains in both world wars, particularly from Southampton Docks over the MSWJ. Freight also reached a peak during wartime, when the junction worked to capacity with a constant procession of essential wartime traffic. By the mid-1950s, there were four southbound through freights over the MSWJ, leaving Cheltenham (High Street) at 4.10am, 6.48am, 12.48pm and 3.20pm for Andover, Eastleigh or Southampton and a local goods at 7.5am, for Swindon Town. In the northbound direction, besides two goods workings from Swindon, there were just two through freights, 11.30am from Bevois Park and 7.4pm from Southampton Docks, which was not due in Cheltenham until 1.2am, so keeping open the signal boxes at Andoversford until the early hours. All these trains disappeared gradually and ceased altogether when Lansdown Junction was altered in November 1958. The pick-up freight from Swindon to Andoversford continued to run until September 1961 and, even after that, the Cheltenham to Kingham pick-up still called at Andoversford and Dowdeswell goods yard until October 1962.

Midland class 3 4-4-0 No. 756 stands at the north end of Lansdown station, with the crew looking back awaiting the 'right away' on an up express. Probably the train has already drawn up as the first two coaches are off the platform. The class 3s were top link power for many years on the line, even into the early LMS period. The rather crude tender cab suggests this was taken in World War 1, when engines had these cabs fitted to reduce the glow from the fire when the firebox door was open, in case of air attack.
A. B. MacLeod Coll/N.R.M. York

MOTIVE POWER

A wide variety of motive power could be observed in steam days in the Cheltenham area. While the most powerful express locomotives in the late LMS and GWR era, such as the 'Duchess' Pacifics and 'King' class 4-6-0s, were not allowed, most other types could work through Cheltenham.

In the early days of the Birmingham & Gloucester, the famous American-built Norris 4-2-0s worked most traffic. In the 1850s, the 2-4-0 type became a familiar sight on the Midland and had a long association with the area, so much so that one of the last was station pilot at Lansdown in 1949, shortly before withdrawal. The beautiful Midland single wheelers were also seen spinning through Cheltenham over the years. Johnson 4-4-0s, including the Class 3 rebuilds, gradually began to take over the most important trains on the Birmingham-Bristol line and were still the top motive power in early LMS days, but Compound 4-4-0s became increasingly familiar throughout the rest of the 1920s. 0-4-4 tanks worked trains to Ashchurch and Great Malvern. Double-framed 0-6-0s worked freights and anything else offered, giving way over the years to Johnson and Fowler 0-6-0s. In the 1930s, modern

power appeared in the form of Stanier 'Black 5' 4-6-0s and then 'Jubilee' Class 3-cylinder 4-6-0s, which remained the top-link power for the rest of the steam era. A rare sighting during Christmas 1946 was an ex London & North Western Railway 'Prince of Wales' 4-6-0 on a down express. Double heading, which was common in Midland days, often still occurred in the BR era on heavy trains such as the Cardiff-Newcastle, with a Compound and 'Jubilee' being a regular combination.

In the 1950s, motive power on the line was fairly settled in the first half of the decade, with 'Jubilees', 'Black 5s', including the Caprotti valve gear members of the class, or the new BR Standard 73XXX class on the main trains, double heading as necessary with Class 2P 4-4-0s or Compounds, which still handled some relief expresses on their own. Semi-fasts and stoppers were handled by the 4-4-0s, though slowly being replaced by BR 75XXX, Ivatt Class 4 2-6-0s, various LMS 2-6-4T and Fowler 0-6-0s, with goods trains in the care of Stanier Class 8F 2-8-0s, 0-6-0s of 3F and 4F, Beyer Garratt 2-6-0+0-6-2 on at least four occasions, and, as they were built in ever increasing numbers, BR 9F

With Lansdown bridge as a background, rebuilt 'Patriot' 4-6-0 No. 45512 Bunsen is a rare visitor, with a train conveying racing pigeons. These trains ran regularly during the season and often produced rare motive power, a boon for local trainspotters. The pigeons only had one-way tickets, they had to fly back to their bases in the North of England. *R. Stanton*

2-10-0s. 'Crab' 2-6-0s tended to appear regularly, often on specific trains, such as the beer from Burton-upon-Trent, also being seen on holiday trains. A solitary unrebuilt 'Patriot', No. 45509 *The Derbyshire Yeomanry,* was, literally, an everyday sight on a morning express from Nottingham to Bristol. Ex-GWR locomotives were regulars on the route on various duties, such as Worcester-Gloucester locals and the Tavistock Junction-Crewe fast freight, although these locos were banned for many years from entering Birmingham New Street station, so could not work through passengers. As the decade progressed, more variations began to appear: LNER B1 4-6-0s steamed through first on occasional excursions but, by 1959, had become common performers, particularly on summer Saturday extras. As diesels started work replacing steam on main lines around the country, previously rarely seen classes, such as 'Royal Scot' and rebuilt 'Patriot' 4-6-0s filtered onto the Birmingham-Bristol line, from their new homes at places like Saltley (Birmingham) and Derby. Three unrebuilt 'Patriots' gravitated to Bristol (Barrow Road) shed and were seen daily. Stanier 2-6-0s in the 429XX series were fairly frequent performers on summer specials. Many unusual visitors have been recorded over the BR years – a few examples, not intended to be exhaustive, follow: Southern Region 'West County' light Pacific; from the Eastern Region J39 0-6-0, both K1 and K3 2-6-0, L1 2-6-4T, O1 2-8-0, V2 2-6-2 and A3 4-6-2 *Flying Scotsman* on railway enthusiast specials; BR Standard 'Clan' 4-6-2; Midland Region ex-LNWR 0-8-0s and ex-Somerset & Dorset 2-8-0s. Engines going to or from works overhaul or transferring depots added more variety, including Deeley 0-4-0T and Kitson 0-4-0ST Dock Shunter, Collett 0-6-0PT of the 1366 class and ex-Lancashire and Yorkshire 0-4-0St

As dieselisation took hold – main line diesel locos were familiar on both the Ashchurch and Honeybourne routes from 1961 onwards and multiple units from some years earlier – some old favourites, such as several of the Bristol 'Jubilees', famed over the years for their performance and cleanliness, were transferred away from the area. In the early 1960s, trains booked for diesel motive power sometimes had steam substitutes, particularly so in the harsh winter of 1962/63, when many diesels froze up over Christmas and something resembling chaos afflicted not just railways, but roads as well, for many weeks. The *Cornishman*, booked for diesel working since transfer to the Ashchurch route in 1962, often turned up with a steam loco, as did the *Devonian* and some of the heaviest trains like the up evening mail from Bristol. The role of steam on the Ashchurch main line declined slowly, rather than disappearing overnight. At the start of the summer service in 1965, local passenger workings between Worcester and Gloucester ceased to be steam and steam on Saturday relief passengers was rare, only two being noted in August, both with 'Black 5' 4-6-0s. However, there were over 20 freight and parcels trains on weekdays scheduled for steam haulage. When the Western Region finished with steam at the end of 1965, steam still worked down from the Midland Region in ever decreasing numbers in 1966, Sunday being the busiest, with freights

from the Midlands. Engines usually went back north light, up to five coupled together, to reduce line occupation. The last commercial working known to the author was on 4 September 1966, when 9F 2-10-0 No. 92094 worked to Gloucester and returned north light engine.

The GWR line from Gloucester to Cheltenham was broad gauge until May 1872. A 'Sun' class 2-2-2 named Rocket was known to be working on the Cheltenham line in the early days, also probably 'Leo' Class 2-4-0, converted to tank locos, as were members of the 'Sun' class. In 1851, four locos were allocated to Cheltenham, and, in 1862, there were six. They were all passenger engines; a 'Victoria' Class 2-4-0; a 'Waverley' Class 4-4-0; and four 'Wolf' Class 4-2-2ST (originally built as 'Star' Class 2-2-2).

Standard gauge GWR locomotives used on local trains on the route were a variety of tank locos, 'Metro' 2-4-0T being prominent for many years, with an 0-6-0ST for shunting duties at St James'. New engines began to appear and 45XX 2-6-2T were prominent in the 1930s. By the end of 1947 the first large 'Prairie' tank, No. 4141, had moved into Malvern Road shed, as had diesel railcar No. 25.

In BR days, Cheltenham St James' to Gloucester passengers, including the through trains to Paddington, could be worked by any engine that happened to be available, but were mainly the province of various 2-6-2T and 0-6-0PT, 2-6-0, Collett's 0-6-0, GWR railcars, 0-6-2T of the 56XX class, 'Manor' 4-6-0s, even 14XX 0-4-2T. BR Standard types also worked the duties, including 82XXX 2-6-2T and Midland engines were not unknown. Steam on the Paddington workings finished on 31 October 1964, with No. 4100 hauling the *Cheltenham Spa Express* from Gloucester Central to St James'. After this date, Paddington trains ran via Gloucester Eastgate, avoiding the need to reverse and were diesel-hauled throughout. The last regular steam working into St James' in 1965 and, indeed, the last steam passenger between Gloucester and Cheltenham, was the 5pm from Gloucester Central, which could produce 'Castle' No. 7029, the last of its class in active use, one day and 0-6-0PT No. 8745 the next, with 'Black 5s' being rostered as well during this period. This working lasted until the closure of St James'.

On the Banbury and Cheltenham, 517 and 3571 Class 0-4-2T and 'Metro' 2-4-0T usually worked the Cheltenham to Kingham locals, while 3521 Class 4-4-0s were still rostered on some workings in the 1920s, until the ubiquitous 2-6-2T took over, with appearances by various 0-6-0PT from time to time, also the occasional 78XXX Class 2-6-0 and 82XXX Class 2-6-2T. The Newcastle to South Wales train over the route had Dean 4-4-0s at the inception, in later days it was usually a 'Mogul' 2-6-0, with 'Manor' 4-6-0s for a short time in the late 1930s before the working disappeared from the timetable. The line also saw Churchward 2-8-0s and Aberdare 2-6-0s on iron ore trains, with 'Dean Goods', 'Barnum' 2-4-0s, various 4-4-0s and Collett 0-6-0s on other freight and special workings. Larger passenger 4-6-0s were not common on the line, although a 'Hall' has been seen on the annual Sunday School excursion from Charlton Kings

and Leckhampton. On Cheltenham race days, 'Castle' 4-6-0s, too large for the St James' turntable, sometimes used the triangle at Gloucester Loop Junction.

The coming of the MSWJ in 1891 introduced various locomotive types from that railway. 2-4-0 tanks by Beyer Peacock of Manchester were used at first – one, No. 6, distinguished itself by leaving the rails at Charlton Kings in September 1891. As the MSWJ was short of engines and cash after the opening to Cheltenham, it sometimes hired locos from the LSWR, but in October 1893, the company took delivery of a fine 4-4-0 from Dubs of Glasgow, No. 9, which set to work on a newly introduced express train to Andover, later through to Southampton, From 1894, it shared these duties with three 2-4-0s, Nos.

10, 11 and 12, from the same builder. For through freight traffic, the MSWJ acquired a Beyer Peacock 2-6-0 in 1895, No. 14, with a second one, No. 16, being delivered two years later. These were similar to locos built for New South Wales and proved to be well up to the task of hauling heavy goods traffic over the grades through the Cotswolds; one was usually based at Cheltenham. No. 14 was taken out of traffic in 1913 and its boiler used at Cheltenham shed for boiler washouts of other locos. Another notable type seen at Lansdown was the 4-4-4 tank, of which there were two, Nos. 17 and 18. Built by Sharp, Stewart of Glasgow, both were stationed at Cheltenham; they were handsome machines, but not very effective, being prone to slip and sometimes needing banking assistance even for light trains on the gradients up to

Andoversford from Cheltenham. Solid work on the MSWJ was performed by the ten 0-6-0s, Nos. 19 to 28, from Beyer Peacock in 1899 and 1902, several being shedded at Cheltenham from new. Finally, the MSWJ purchased nine inside cylinder 4-4-0s between 1905 and 1914 from the North British Locomotive Company. These were very successful, being used on passengers and fast freights, with most being allocated to Cheltenham. Various engines from other railways worked through on military traffic in World War 1, including K10 and T9 4-4-0s of the LSWR and Class 2 4-4-0s of the Midland, while the latter's Class 2 and 3 0-6-0s were employed on various duties. A number of the MSWJ engines were heavily rebuilt by the GWR after the grouping and the later 4-4-0s and the 0-6-0s continued to work on the line for a few years, although GWR built locos slowly took over services. 'Duke' 4-4-0s were at first the largest GWR passenger engines allowed on the line, while Collett's 22XX Class gradually appeared. Then GWR 2-6-0s and 'Manor' Class 4-6-0s worked services, the latter being based at Cheltenham (Malvern Road) into the 1950s specifically to work MSWJ trains. Southern Region 'U' Class 2-6-0s appeared in Cheltenham from around 1953, often twice a day – as one arrived about 1.35pm in Lansdown on the 10.10am from Southampton, another would be waiting to leave on the 1.56pm back home. Southern Region BR Standard classes of 75XXX 4-6-0 and 76XXX 2-6-0 also traversed the line in the 1950s and up to closure. Towards the end of the line's existence, 'N' Class 2-6-0s put in more frequent appearances. Various other types turned up occasionally in BR days, one of the most notable being T9 4-4-0 No. 30288 on the 10.10am from Southampton and the return 3.20pm freight to Eastleigh, while Q and Q1 Class 0-6-0s have been observed on special freights. Regular through freights were often handled by WD 2-8-0s, GWR 2-8-0s and 2-6-0s, also Collett 0-6-0s.

In the early years of the Honeybourne line, steam railmotors were used on stopping trains to and from Cheltenham. They were allocated to Malvern Road shed until 1918, but were replaced by push-and-pull fitted 0-4-2T on one or two trailers, as well as 0-6-0PT, 2-4-0T and 2-6-2T on conventional passenger trains. When through expresses started in 1908, inside cylinder 4-4-0s of 'Atbara', 'Badminton', 'Flower' and 'County' classes worked these trains. Due to weight restrictions elsewhere, it was 1927 before 'Saint' 4-6-0s appeared and, later, 'Castles' became familiar through to the end of steam. Most other GWR classes of 4-6-0, except 'Kings', were regulars and, in latter days, ex-LMS and BR 4-6-0s were common. Even ex-LNER B1 4-6-0s were not unknown, on trains diverted from the route through Ashchurch. Also, in 1965, up to three BR 'Britannia' 4-6-2s a day were seen on summer Saturday specials. And, of course, the GWR 'maids of all work', the 43XX 2-6-0s worked anything and everything. The Honeybourne line was also one of the first to have diesel railcars, from 9 July 1934. From late 1941, the twin railcar sets, with a centre coach added, ran on the line, whenever loadings were within their capacity, but gradually gave way to steam hauled services. Most of these, in turn, were replaced by modern diesel multiple units in 1957/58, leaving the *Cornishman* as the only daily steam express on the line, apart from specials. Ironically, perhaps, steam passenger on this line just outlasted that on the ex-LMS line through Ashchurch, the 12.30pm Penzance to Wolverhampton being booked for steam for the last time on 4 September 1965, with the only 'Castle' still in service, No. 7029, *Clun*

Castle based at Gloucester (Horton Road).

Freight trains were handled by 'Aberdare' 2-6-0s, 43XX Moguls, Churchward 2-8-0s, ex-ROD 2-8-0s and various 4-6-0s, with local traffic seeing Collett 0-6-0s and, sometimes, 4-4-0s. 2-8-0T and 2-8-2T also appeared, while Stanier's 2-8-0s were frequent, as were ex-WD 2-8-0s and, from the mid-1950s, BR 2-10-0s of the 92XXX class. The Honeybourne pick-up had small and large GWR 0-6-0PT, also 2-6-2T, and BR Standard 2-6-0s of the 78XXX class. Steam was still quite active on the line in 1965 on iron ore and other freights, but by 1966 the steamiest action was on Sundays, when backlogs of goods trains were worked down from the Midlands. Probably the final regular steam working on the route in summer 1966, lasting into August, was a parcels train from Birmingham (Snow Hill) to Swindon which went through the now-closed Malvern Road at around 11.15pm, usually with a 'Black 5' 4-6-0, often No. 44780, returning in the early hours with a parcels train for Moor Street, Birmingham.

On the Ashchurch to Malvern line, Gloucester Barnwood shed provided engines, which also shunted at Ashchurch and worked local turns on the Evesham line. Through trains from the Birmingham area via Evesham were worked by engines supplied by Saltley and Bourneville sheds. A Kirtley 0-4-4 well tank worked on the Malvern line, along with 0-6-0s by the same designer and Johnson engines of the same wheel arrangements. No. 58071, with Salter safety valves right up to its withdrawal in the 1950s, was the last Johnson 0-4-4T to be associated with the branch. Even then, the type was not finished, as Stanier 0-4-4T No.41900 worked the branch in the late 1950s, being the last of its class at work. In the early 1950s, two others of the class, Nos. 41902 and 41903 also worked in the area. Other types to be seen at Tewkesbury shed during the LMS and BR years were, on workings from the Malvern and Evesham lines, Deeley 0-6-4T, Class 2 and 4 4-4-0s, Class 2, 3 and 4 0-6-0s, 'Jinty' 0-6-0T, Fowler and Stanier 2-6-2T and 2-6-4T, while Ivatt Class 2 2-6-0 No. 46401 was a regular performer on the Upton service, as were Ivatt Class 4 2-6-0 on the Evesham line. During the war years, Birmingham based engines were often stabled at Tewkesbury, to keep them out of harm's way in case of air raids on their home city. A slightly different working noted in the 1950s was a BR Standard 73XXX on Tewkesbury shed being fitted with a new speedometer by the Smiths Industries factory at Bishops Cleeve near Cheltenham. When the Western Region took over responsibility for the shed in the late 1950s, 77XX Class 0-6-0PT were often in use on both lines. Until 9 September 1960, the loco off a freight working from Washwood Heath, Birmingham, to Evesham ran light engine to Tewkesbury shed for servicing, which brought in 'Black 5' 4-6-0s and Stanier 2-8-0s. Almost at the end of this working, on 8 September, the loco was ex-LNWR 0-8-0 No. 49106, a fairly rare visitor. Other engines coming in for servicing at this time were off: the morning passenger from Redditch to Ashchurch; the Upton passenger; the Evesham pick-up freight and the 5.10pm passenger from Birmingham New Street to Ashchurch via Evesham. On 8 September, the four locos involved were Nos. 42416, 47539, 47422 and 42417, while by contrast, on 12 May that year, they were Nos. 42327 (whose return working was taken by No. 44264), 7756, 43645 and 43012, with No. 42791 turning up off the Washwood Heath turn. So, even at a small shed like Tewkesbury, there was a fair variety of motive power.

Stanier 0-4-4T No. 41900 was a well-known performer on the Ashchurch-Upton on Severn branch in the late 1950s, but less known is that Nos. 41901 and 41902 were here in the early years of that decade. No.41902 is shunting on the down side at Ashchurch in 1950. *W. Potter*

World War 2 produced engines from the Southern Railway and LNER in the area to help out with the heavy traffic requirements. LNER Class B12 4-6-0s, used because of their light axle load, appeared on hospital trains over the MSWJ line, sometimes doubleheaded. A lot of hospital trains went along the Ashchurch-Malvern line and were usually hauled by two engines. LNER 0-6-0s of the J25 Class were shedded in the area for shunting and trip work. Ex LSWR 4-4-0s of Classes K10 and S11 were also stationed in the area and could be seen around Ashchurch and Cheltenham. The new Ministry of Supply WD 2-8-0s became familiar, as did the American built United States Army Transportation Corps (USATC) 2-8-0s; for example, five of the type were seen at Lansdown Junction one evening in September 1944. The latter engines often worked in to the newly constructed Ashchurch army depot, which, in August 1944, had three USATC 0-6-0T for internal shunting.

There have been three locomotive depots in Cheltenham. The first was at St George's Road and was originally broad gauge, opened in October 1847, being later converted to standard. In 1901 it had an allocation of seven locomotives, six 'Metro' 2-4-0T and one 0-6-0ST When the Honeybourne line was constructed, this depot was in the way, so it was demolished and a new two road brick shed built at Malvern Road in 1906. The allocation was nine engines in 1921 (including, still, six 'Metro' tanks) and 13 in 1938. Despite this increase in numbers, caused by the closure of the ex-MSWJ shed at High Street, Malvern Road was downgraded from a main shed to a sub-shed of Gloucester in 1935. An extension was added and by the end of 1947, the shed had 17 locos, including a diesel railcar. In later years, LMS 2-6-4T off the Evesham-Ashchurch line passenger appeared on a turn covered by Malvern Road men when Tewkesbury shed lost its crews in August 1961. By this time, Malvern Road was also being used

to store engines, including 'Grange' Class 4-6-0 and LMS 4F 0-6-0. For a brief time in the late 1950s and early 1960s, the shed had diesel refuelling facilities, but these were removed even before closure of the shed in October 1963.

The MSWJ constructed its shed at High Street in 1893, just a simple single road affair in the early years, while a turntable had been put in place outside Lansdown station. With an allocation of ten engines in 1902, space was at a premium and, eventually, a solid three road brick shed was built, which came into use in December 1911. Various members of the MSWJ fleet were stationed here over the years; a couple of the 2-4-0s; a 2-6-0, both the 4-4-4T, around five or six 0-6-0 and most of the 4-4-0, with 0-4-4T No. 15 also being here at times. Midland Railway engines on local duties were also stabled here. After the grouping, the GW types which gradually supplanted the 0-6-0s and 4-4-0s also used the shed when they were on MSWJ duties. The depot finally closed in December 1935, with engines and duties transferred to Malvern Road, Remarkably both Malvern Road and the 1911 High Street shed still exist in 1993, though neither are in railway use.

On an everyday basis, two Gloucester sheds, the GWR's Horton Road and the Midland's Barnwood supplied many of the engines seen passing through Cheltenham. On the Ashchurch main line, through express engines were based at places such as Bristol, Derby and Leeds, with Birmingham's Saltley and Bourneville sheds providing power for lesser workings. Wolverhampton (Stafford Road) and Birmingham Tyseley usually provided for expresses on the Honeybourne line, while GWR engines from various South Wales sheds were regular performers on freight duties, as were locos from the ex Great Central Railway depot at Woodford Halse. In later years, Eastleigh on the Southern Region sent its engines over the old MSWJ on regular duties.

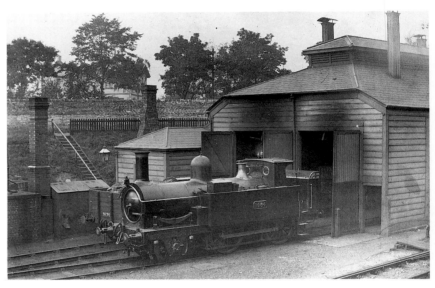

The first GWR loco shed in Cheltenham was originally broad gauge and was situated at St George's Road, until it was demolished to make way for the Honeybourne line. This fine photograph shows clearly the wooden construction. 'Metro' tank No. 1404 awaits its next duty, possibly to Gloucester or on the Kingham line.   *D. Bick Coll*

This three road loco shed was built at High Street by the MSWJ and came into use in July 1911; it replaced an earlier single road wooden shed. In December 1934, more than ten years after the GWR had taken it over, ex MSWJ 4-4-0 No. 1, now GWR No. 1119, simmers at its home shed awaiting the next duty to Southampton. The loco had already been rebuilt twice by the GWR – it had been fitted with one of the MSWJ double-domed boilers in the 1920s, reverting to a single-domed boiler in 1932. Alongside is GWR 'Dean Goods' 0-6-0 No. 2517, presumably also employed on MSWJ line services. The shed closed in 1935, but the building still survives in 1993, though not in railway service.   *W. Potter*

CHURCHDOWN AND BADGEWORTH

Churchdown station, looking towards Gloucester, a view believed to date from the early years of this century. The station was treated as a joint station by the Midland and GWR. It opened to passengers on 2 February 1874 and was the second station at Churchdown, the first being a very short lived affair in 1842. As mentioned elsewhere, the line from Gloucester Tramway Junction to Churchdown was maintained by the Midland and from there to Cheltenham Lansdown Junction by the Great Western.   *Lens of Sutton*

Looking towards Cheltenham as a Midland 4-4-0 passes through on the Bournemouth express, a train destined to traverse the Somerset and Dorset Railway from Bath to Bournemouth. Major changes occurred at Churchdown with the widening to four tracks in 1942.   *Lens of Sutton*

This view on 28 December 1957 shows two main lines through the middle of the station, while two relief lines have been added on the outside of the platforms. There have been various changes to the buildings and the signal box, of a standard outline, was opened on 28 June 1942, just before the relief lines came into operation. The train here is an extra express to Paignton, hauled by Sheffield based 4-6-0 No. 45056, heading towards Gloucester.

B. W. L. Brooksbank

Another down additional express, on the relief line this time, steams through, from Wolverhampton Low Level to Bristol and Penzance, behind 'Castle' 4-6-0 No. 7026 *Tenby Castle* on 24 June 1961.

J. Dagley-Morris

Although built as freight locomotives, BR class 9F 2-10-0s were often pressed into service on passenger trains in the area; on 20 August 1960, Cardiff (Canton) based No. 92237 runs through on the up main line with the 8.30am Pembroke Dock to Birmingham (Snow Hill) passenger. *B. W. L. Brooksbank*

Diesel power on other parts of BR released a number of 'Royal Scot' 4-6-0s to work trains in the area in the early 1960s – previously sightings of this type had been rare – and a clean No. 46157 *The Royal Artilleryman* of Saltley (Birmingham) shed heads the regular 10.20am Bristol Temple Meads-Newcastle through Churchdown on 24 June 1961.

J. Dagley-Morris

Through trains from London (Paddington) to Cheltenham Spa (St. James') usually had a glamorous 'Castle' 4-6-0 to Gloucester (Central), but for the last few miles to Cheltenham, the motive power was rather more humble, varying from 2-6-2 tanks to small tender locos and even smaller 0-6-0 pannier tanks, with a full complement of ten or so coaches. Here is another variation, one of Gloucester's 0-6-2T, No. 6696, on the 9.5am from Paddington, the date being 4 November 1961.

B. W. L. Brooksbank

2-6-2T No. 4573 heads away from Churchdown towards Cheltenham with the train from London on 29 August 1959.
R. Dagley-Morris

The area had possibly more than its share of superannuated engines working out their final days, as illustrated here by Gloucester's 'Duke' class 4-4-0 No. 9064 *Trevithick,* one of the last survivors of the class, on a short northbound freight near Churchdown on 30 July 1949.
B. W. L. Brooksbank

The next signal box north of Churchdown was at Badgeworth, and in the era of two lines, ex-ROD now GWR 2-8-0 No. 3026 takes a wartime freight towards Badgeworth bridge and Gloucester in October 1940.   *W. Potter*

Badgeworth signal box is visible in this July 1941 view of 'Saint' class 4-6-0 No. 2905 *Lady Macbeth* on an up local passenger train.   *W. Potter*

Virtually the same viewpoint on 3 August 1957 – now with four tracks and a new type signal box – as again a stopping passenger train, the 7.30am Swansea to St. James' goes past in charge of 0-6-0PT No. 9441. Included in the rake is a GWR Centenary coach, reduced from glamorous expresses to stopping trains. Behind the passenger is a 4F 0-6-0 running up light engine on the relief line.

B. W. L. Brooksbank

HATHERLEY AND REDDINGS

Another train from Paddington traverses the Reddings on 3 September 1960 double-headed by 0-6-0PTs Nos. 9477 and 9453. The sun shines on the cleanliness of No. 9453, making an even more pronounced contrast with the grubby No. 9477. The train hardly needs two engines, presumably one engine was working in for other duties.   *R. Dagley-Morris*

In the height of summer Saturday service, freight engine No. 44128 of Gloucester (Barnwood) depot has been commandeered to haul a Rotherham to Paignton relief train on 23 July 1960. It has just passed under the footbridge near the Old Reddings Road. Adjacent to the railway here was an extensive earth mound, excavated when the railway was widened from two to four tracks in 1942. The 88 milepost in the foreground is the distance to Derby, headquarters of the Midland Railway.   *J. Dagley-Morris*

An interesting picture at Hatherley bridge during the widening. A new bridge is under construction on the up side while sleepers are being laid ready to receive the track. The four track layout here came into use on 9 August 1942. *M. P. Barnsley Coll*

In 1948 'Jubilee' 4-6-0 No. 5636 *Uganda* approaches Hatherley bridge on a northbound express going through Lansdown station. It is on the up main line and will cross to the up relief beyond Cloddymore bridge to gain entry to the Midland station. *E. R. Morten*

The photographer then crossed to the other side of the bridge and took a busy scene at Hatherley Junction, quite typical of the level of activity on this important main line. As No. 5636 heads for Cloddymore, 'Black 5' No. 5040 comes down the main line from Cheltenham with another express and a goods train occupies the up relief. The relatively new Hatherley signal box seen here was built in 1942 when the line was quadrupled. The short line to Gloucester Loop Junction, which curves off in front of the box, was already bereft of regular traffic by 1948, but remained open for occasional use.

E. R. Morten

Ex-LNER Class B1 4-6-0s became familiar visitors in the late 1950s and here is No. 61164 on a summer Bournemouth to Leicester working on 27 June 1959 approaching Hatherley bridge with the signal at caution.   *R. Dagley-Morris*

An unusual working on 11 October 1960 has 'Jinty' 0-6-0T No. 47422 on an up freight at Hatherley. This loco was often shunter at Cheltenham (High Street) goods yard and stabled at Malvern Road shed between turns. Its home shed was Gloucester (Barnwood) and its trips there and back were usually light engine.
J. Dagley-Morris

The pre-nationalisation spirit of rivalry between GWR and LMS enginemen was often still apparent on the line. The signalman at Hatherley captures the race in the early 1960s as 4-6-0 No. 6803 *Bucklebury Grange* on a short fast freight tries to catch up 'Royal Scot' No. 46164 *The Artists' Rifleman* on an up express.

R. Stanton

A double-headed express storms past Hatherley box in charge of Caprotti valve gear class 5 4-6-0 No. 44754 of Leeds (Holbeck) shed and Bristol (Barrow Road) 'Jubilee' 4-6-0 No. 45660 *Rooke* on 8 April 1961. The train is the 10.30am Bristol (Temple Meads)-Newcastle. A few years previously, the pilot engine would have been an ex-Midland 2P or Compound 4-4-0.
J. Dagley-Morris

Ex-Midland 0-6-0 No. 43521 trundles a loose-coupled mixed freight down the main towards Gloucester on 10 June 1961 past Hatherley box. This class did many years sterling service in the area and were well regarded for their strength and free steaming abilities. Across from the railway new houses on the Benhall estate begin to change the rural nature of the area.
J. Dagley-Morris

The last vestiges of the junction at Hatherley are being removed as five engines – of five different classes – return home on a Sunday. This was a fairly common sight in the early-to-mid sixties, when backlogs of freight from the north were cleared on Sundays, with no corresponding back workings. *R. Stanton*

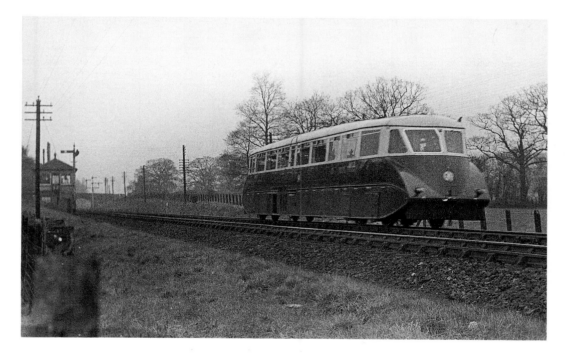

CLODDYMORE CROSSING

Top: In the days of two tracks from Gloucester to Cheltenham, here is a fine portrait of Midland Compound No. 1028 on a Bristol-York express approaching Cloddymore crossing on 18 March 1933. *E. R. Morten*

Bottom: A new GWR diesel railcar, No. 2, invades the steam era on 7 March 1935, as it makes for St. James'. These railcars became a familiar sight – in 1936 there was a Swindon Junction - Gloucester - Cheltenham - Cirencester Watermoor - Swindon Junction working, as well as, at various times, local trains from Gloucester to Cheltenham, an express service from Swansea to Cheltenham and a single railcar, in later years a three-car set, operating from Birmingham (Snow Hill) to South Wales. Hatherley signal box in the background was removed for further use in Exeter when the new box was built in 1942. *E. R. Morten*

A local train to St. James' on the up main comes under Cloddymore bridge on 14 September 1955, hauled by No. 5514, a regular performer. The signals show a train is due on the down main, which must be coming from Malvern Road, otherwise there will be a nasty accident at Lansdown Junction, where No. 5514 will travel across the down line from Lansdown station.

E. R. Morten

This is the down train signalled, and it has, indeed, come out of Malvern Road, being the down *Cornishman,* hauled, as normal, by a Wolverhampton based 'Castle' 4-6-0.

E. R. Morten

On 6 June 1961, unrebuilt 'Patriot' No. 45506 *Royal Pioneer Corps* waits on the up relief with the 8.50am Bristol (St. Philips Marsh) to Water Orton part-fitted express freight as BR Standard 4-6-0 No. 75022 overtakes on the 11.30am Gloucester (Eastgate) to Birmingham (New Street) passenger. Both trains will traverse Lansdown station. *J. Dagley-Morris*

On 26 September 1961, 0-6-2T No. 6696 waits at signals on a Gloucester to Cheltenham local for 4F 0-6-0 No. 44272 to cross Lansdown Junction on a down semi-fitted goods. *J. Dagley-Morris*

Below: Hughes 2-6-0 No. 42784 has a clear run into Lansdown Station on a summer extra, in a view looking back beyond Cloddymore towards Hatherley bridge. The most important regular train for this class was the down evening Burton beer – a lovely sight for steam and beer lovers . . *J. Dagley-Morris*

A double-framed Midland 0-6-0 hauls a mixed goods towards Lansdown bridge in the early years of the century. Although the front of the engine is unfortunately blurred, it does show a good view of the Banbury line junction (on the other side of the bridge was the Honeybourne line junction). The two lines on the left head for Andoversford on the GWR, also used by the MSWJ who had running powers over the line. The two lines on the right are the joint GWR-MR lines to Gloucester. Cloddy crossing is past the back of the train and, on the left, is Dean Close public school. The hut behind the van is the approximate location of the Lansdown Junction signal box, built many years later in 1942, when the railway to Gloucester was widened from two to four tracks. *A. B. MacLeod Coll/N.R.M. York*

LANSDOWN JUNCTION

In the early post-war years, a GWR 2-6-0 eases off the Andoversford line towards Lansdown station on a working from Andover or Southampton. Taken from Lansdown Bridge, the photo shows the changes wrought by the 1942 widening.
E. R. Morten

GWR 4-6-0 No. 6804 *Brockington Grange* heads an express freight towards Lansdown station off the up main on 14 September 1955. *E. R. Morten*

The premier train on the ex-LMS Bristol-Birmingham line was the *Devonian,* from Paignton to Bradford. On 28 June 1958 Bristol 'Jubilee' 4-6-0 No. 45662 *Kempenfelt* coast towards Lansdown station – although it did not stop at Cheltenham, it had to slow down for the sharp curve through the station. The northbound *Devonian* passed at about 1.30pm and the southbound around 3pm.

E. R. Morten

There was a stopping train service from Hereford and here is the 4pm from that cathedral city heading for Malvern Road and St. James' with 0-6-0 No. 2249 as motive power. This was on 25 August 1962 and shows Lansdown Junction after removal of the connections from Lansdown station to the Andoversford line. *J. Dagley-Morris*

Three views inside Lansdown Junction box – this was a very busy place and, in the 1950s at least, had a booking boy to log trains, as well as the duty signalmen.   *R. Stanton*

This photo, taken from Lansdown Junction signal box, shows Southern Region Class U 2-6-0 No. 31621 of Eastleigh depot hauling the 3.20pm Cheltenham (High Street) to Southampton goods in the late 1950s. The engine arrived around 1.35pm at Lansdown station on the passenger from Southampton. The connection from Lansdown, shown here, was removed in November 1958, not only virtually ending through freight onto the old MSWJ route, but really sealing its fate.

R. Stanton

The first station along the Kingham line was Leckhampton and here is an undated view. When the Newcastle on Tyne to South Wales train started to call here in 1906, the station name changed to Cheltenham South and Leckhampton to emphasise that the service had a stop at Cheltenham, albeit on the outskirts.

Lens of Sutton

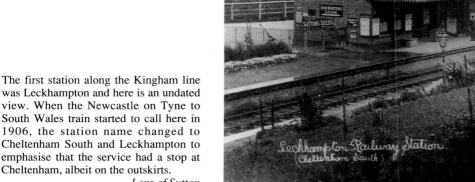

LECKHAMPTON

In post-war years, the station name became Cheltenham Leckhampton, as shown in this view, taken on 26 November 1960, looking south.   *E. Wilmshurst*

Just a month before services were withdrawn, 2-6-2T No. 4100 stands in Cheltenham Leckhampton station on a Kingham passenger, the date being 15 September 1962.   *W. Potter*

The pick-up freight, 8.10am from Cheltenham (St. James') to Kingham, on Mondays, Wednesdays and Fridays only by this time, blasts through Leckhampton on 15 March 1961, hauled by 0-6-0PT No. 9453. It was scheduled to shunt at Leckhampton, Andoversford, Notgrove, Bourton-on-the-Water and Stow-on-the-Wold, arriving in Kingham at 12.33pm. Not much time was scheduled at Kingham, departure from there being at 12.55pm, due back in St. James's at 3.35pm.

J. Dagley-Morris

2-6-0 No. 7341 pulls a pigeon special past Pilley bridge in Leckhampton on 20 May 1961. The train was journeying from Chesterfield to Andover, hence was destined to travel over the MSWJ. There is evidence of some track re-laying in this section. Pilley bridge suffered wartime damage as the result of a direct hit from the Luftwaffe.

J. Dagley-Morris

CHELTENHAM SOUTH & LECKHAMPTON SIGNAL BOX

CHARLTON KINGS

Charlton Kings station, looking towards Andoversford, on May 9 1954.

W. Potter

Looking the other way towards Cheltenham on 3 October 1960 finds Southern Region 2-6-0 No. 31803 of Eastleigh shed arriving on the 1.52pm Cheltenham Spa (St. James') - Southampton Terminus, by this date the only southbound train connecting the two places. The platform is looking a little neglected with weeds growing through. *J. Dagley-Morris*

A superbly atmospheric shot of the afternoon Cheltenham-Kingham passenger steaming through Charlton Kings on 10 November 1960, behind 2-6-2T No. 8107. *J. Dagley-Morris*

Here is a rare wartime photo, taken behind the Reservoir Inn outside Charlton Kings in May 1944. The locomotive, of unfamiliar outline, is a United States Army Transportation Corps 2-8-0, many of which were loaned to British railways to cope with war traffic. The line up to Andoversford and on to Andover and Southampton was extremely busy during the war, and with D-Day not far away, the line would probably have been working to capacity.

W. Potter

In June 1945, a heavy goods train runs down towards Cheltenham with impressive motive power – 2-8-2T No. 7246 and 2-8-0 No.2867. The reservoir and Dowdeswell viaduct can be seen in the background.

W. Potter

Again with the reservoir behind, 2-6-2T No. 4571 drifts down on the Kingham-Cheltenham local. These small Prairie tanks were prominent on the service for many years, though mainly giving way to the larger Prairies in later years. *W. Potter*

Dowdeswell viaduct, built of red brick with twelve arches, is shown on 2 September 1961 as No. 31794 crosses on the 1.52pm St. James'-Southampton. Only single line originally, it was widened to take two tracks with the advent of the MSWJ. Despite having a particularly pleasing effect on the landscape, it was regrettably demolished in the mid 1960s.
W. Potter

On 4 April 1959, U Class 2-6-0 No. 31807 emerges from Sandywell Park tunnel outside Andoversford into a deeply wooded cutting with the morning passenger from Andover Junction.   *R. Dagley-Morris*

This charming study was taken at Sandywell Park tunnel on 12 August 1914 – it seems as if the local scout troop has been enlisted to help guard the tunnel against invasion from foreign forces, this, of course, being during World War 1. Hopefully they were able to move quickly in the event of invasion by a GWR or MSWJ train. *M.P. Barnsley Coll*

AROUND ANDOVERSFORD

Andoversford station in the BR era, looking towards Cheltenham. Beyond the main building on the left can be seen the goods shed, starter signal, water column and goods sidings. The line from here to Cheltenham was widened from one to two tracks in 1900. *M.P. Barnsley Coll*

There was still a fair amount of freight activity in the 1950s and 2-6-0 No. 5318 runs in past Andoversford Station Signal Box on 28 March 1956. This was probably destined to travel along the ex-MSWJ. *E. R. Morten*

In BR days the main passenger service ran from St. James' to Kingham and the afternoon train is seen here with typical motive power for the time in the form of old favourite No. 4141, which spent virtually its entire working life based at Malvern Road shed. This train is the 9.50am to Kingham, on 11 October 1960. *J. Dagley-Morris*

U Class No. 31801 arrives over the MSWJ junction and crosses the main A40 London road with the 7.50am Andover Junction to Cheltenham (St. James') on 11 October 1960. The lines to the left go to Kingham which was single track all the way; trains could cross at Notgrove and Bourton-on-the-Water stations, but not at Stow-on-the-Wold station. Andoversford Junction signal box is partly obscured on the left edge of the photo. The MSWJ had also been single line only since 1928. *J. Dagley-Morris*

Top: Out in the Cotswolds, at Hampen between Andoversford and Notgrove, 0-6-0PT No. 8743 is deputising for a Prairie tank on the Kingham local in August 1961.

D. Bick

TOWARDS KINGHAM

Middle: Notgrove had the distinction of being the highest GWR station on a through route – over 760 feet above sea level. It was also the summit of 1 in 60 gradients from either direction. This photo was taken in the severe winter of 1962/63, after the line had shut down; station nameboards have gone, but signals and tracks are still in place. The high bridge in the background carries the Andoversford to Bourton-on-the-Water road. The view certainly shows the bleakness of the location and, of course, the snow and drifts would have been worse after a fresh fall than shown here, calling for the passage of the snowplough along the line. *R. Stanton*

A special working late in the line's life occurred on 5 July 1962, when an excursion for the Women's Institute ran from Somersham in East Anglia to Cheltenham and Gloucester. It presumably worked cross-country from Cambridge to Yarnton Junction, near Oxford, then to Kingham. Motive power, seen here near Notgrove, was also unusual for the line, BR 9F 2-10-0 No. 92240 on eight coaches, including several Gresley examples. The excursion returned the same way later in the day.

J. Dagley-Morris

BOURTON-ON-THE-WATER

Top: A view of the original Bourton-on-the-Water station, opened in 1862 and replaced in the early 1930s. The undated picture, looking towards Kingham, is a delightfully busy study of a rural station, when the railway was crucial to the local economy. The locomotive appears to be a 'Metro' 2-4-0T, which were regular performers in pre- and early post-grouping days. *Lens of Sutton*

Bottom: Well into the BR era and the replacement station building, a local freight arrives from Kingham behind 0-6-0 No. 2254. It makes an interesting comparison with the previous photograph. *Lens of Sutton*

Near the end of passenger services, just over one hundred years after trains first ran to Bourton on 1 March 1862, 2-6-2T No. 5184 pauses by the water tank with the 10.50am stopper from Cheltenham on 29 September 1962, having crossed the 11.18am from Kingham hauled by No. 4101.   *H. Ballantyne*

Stow-on-the-Wold only ever had a single platform, even after the station was rebuilt in the early 1930s. This old picture shows the original station, with probably all the staff on duty standing on the platform. A corrugated iron goods shed and a signal box were later built alongside the station. The wagon in the right-hand corner suggests that engineering work might be in progress – but there are what appear to be two passengers standing at the door of the waiting room.   *Lens of Sutton*

STOW-ON-THE-WOLD

ON THE MSWJ

Top: About five-eighths of a mile from Andoversford Junction on the MSWJ line was Andoversford and Dowdeswell, the station that railway used when it was denied access to the GWR's station at Andoversford. It did, in fact, remain in use as a passenger station until 1927, after that, the building became a cafe serving the adjacent A40 road. The goods yard continued in operation, outliving the demise of the MSWJ in September 1961, eventually shutting on the closure of the Kingham line in October 1962. On 21 October 1960, the Cheltenham to Kingham pick-up shunts in the goods yard with 0-6-0PT No. 9727. The goods shed is on the left; behind the wagons were cattle pens, and the weigh bridge. *J. Dagley-Morris*

Bottom: One week later, on 28 October 1960, motive power is provided by 0-6-0PT No. 8409. The train has run up from Andoversford Junction and is standing on the wrong line as was necessary to gain access to the yard. It looks as if the shunter and guard are about to uncouple some wagons to go into the yard. When shunting had finished, presumably the train propelled back to Andoversford Junction and on towards Kingham. As the 7.50am passenger from Andover was due about the time this exercise took place, it was a busy period in this otherwise sleepy spot. *J. Dagley-Morris*

Above: No. 31793 steams past the remains of the closed MSWJ station at Andoversford and Dowdeswell with the Cheltenham-Southampton passenger on 28 March 1959. The line on the left was by this time only used for trains shunting into the goods yard.   *J. Dagley-Morris*

Left: This portrait of Withington station on 16 November 1960 shows a special DMU working from Swindon to Andoversford – probably a running in turn after attention at Swindon Works. Brand new DMUs built at Swindon Works were often tested on a Swindon - Gloucester - Cheltenham - Andoversford - Swindon circuit. Indeed, ex-works steam locos were also familiar on the line in the 1950s, often used on the 5.30pm Cheltenham - Swindon Town passenger service – examples which come to mind include Nos. 2222, 3666 and 6309. The view here is looking north and the station is now an unstaffed halt.   *J. Dagley-Morris*

Bottom: The U Class, this time No. 31791, on the Cheltenham - Southampton train near Withington became a familiar sight over the years – but it is 9 September 1961, the last day of the service and this is the last through train. No headboard or additional coaches mark the event, though there are a few more passengers than normal and someone is waving to the photographer from the front coach. There were enthusiast specials the next day and then silence fell over the railway.   *J. Dagley-Morris*

At Chedworth, there were still a few weeks service left when this photo of the afternoon train to Southampton was taken on 14 June 1961. The station here had been an unstaffed halt since 1 February 1954 and there had only been one line through the station since July 1928.

J. Dagley-Morris

MSWJ 4-4-0s had long since disappeared from the scene, but the Midland Region could still muster 4-4-0s in some quantity and Nos. 40489 and 40454 found use on this enthusiast's railtour from Nottingham to Swindon Works via Cheltenham and the MSWJ on 6 May 1956. The train is steaming through Chedworth and makes a fine sight. No. 40489 was a Gloucester (Barnwood) engine and had been attached at Lansdown as pilot engine over the steep grades. Several engines of this class worked over the MSWJ during World War 1.

H. Ballantyne

FOSS CROSS

The goods yard at Foss Cross closed at the same time as the passenger station, that is on and from 11 September 1961. On 14 June 1961, 2-6-2T No. 5555, a Swindon based engine, draws the pick-up freight from that place on its way to Andoversford Junction. The station building is behind the train, and goods shed to the far left, in the sidings. The standard GWR single line token apparatus is seen on both sides of the track and the up starter signal is also prominent.

J. Dagley-Morris

GWR 'Manor' Class 4-6-0s were a feature of the MSWJ line for some years and were shedded at Cheltenham (Malvern Road) specifically for the route. Until the late 1950s, a 'Manor' worked the daily 10am Cheltenham (Lansdown) to Southampton passenger train, arriving back in Cheltenham at about 8pm. No. 7808 *Cookham Manor* comes home through Foss Cross one summer evening in 1956, with a respectable 6-coach train. *D. Bick*

LANSDOWN STATION

A passenger on Lansdown station in this view, taken about 1900, would have no difficulty in recognising the station today. Lamps have changed, there are no milk churns now and not as many pretty hats, but the basic shape and structure remain the same. The station name became Cheltenham Spa (Lansdown) in February 1925.

B. Matthews Coll

Photographed from Lansdown bridge after widening, a down express departs Lansdown in charge of BR Standard Class 5 4-6-0 No. 73068. The connection to Andoversford was still extant, as reflected by the signals on the gantry. From left to right, these signalled trains from Lansdown to: down main to Gloucester; down relief to Gloucester; up to Andoversford. This sequence was repeated on the signals out of Malvern Road, on the right.

E. R. Morten

Station pilot duties at Lansdown seemed to be a haven for ancient locomotives from Gloucester Barnwood depot. On 9 April 1949, ex-Midland 2F 0-6-0 No. 3062, later to become BR No. 58206 stands in the down bay. The engine lasted well and often worked engineers trains in its latter days. The bay platforms were used by MSWJ passenger trains and this continued after the 1923 grouping.
W. Potter

In the bay again, with Queen's Road in the background, and the main station building behind the loco, is 0-4-4T No. 1251 (BR No. 58034). The engine is shunting a horse-box, possibly in connection with Cheltenham races. Apparently the bay was known as the 'horse-box bay' or 'Ladies College bay'! *W. Potter*

Special enthusiast trains ran through from time to time, and this one, organised by the Gloucestershire Railway Society in 1961, has a particularly appropriate preserved locomotive. Midland Compound No. 1000 was a former resident of Gloucester (Barnwood) shed and so was very familiar in these parts; indeed, the last working Compound, No. 41123, was also at Barnwood, and worked regularly through Cheltenham.
D. Bick

Seen from a vantage point near the bay at Lansdown station, 2-6-2T No. 6137 accelerates away from Lansdown Junction towards Malvern Road station with the 1.25pm Kingham-St. James' on 14 July 1962. On the signal gantry, signals from Lansdown station to Andoversford have gone and, from Malvern Road, the distant signal for the Kingham line has been removed.   *E. Wilmshurst*

An impressive scene at Lansdown station, as 'Jubilee' Class 4-6-0 No. 45682 *Trafalgar* arrives on a northbound express, while its shedmate at Bristol (Barrow Road), 'Patriot' No. 45504 *Royal Signals,* brews up a storm on a down goods.   *J. Dagley-Morris*

Kettering based BR 9F 2-10-0 No. 92089 steams northwards on a mixed goods train with livestock in the first few wagons. In the background another goods train heads out of Malvern Road towards Lansdown Junction. *R. Wales*

Standing at the up platform in Lansdown on a local train, 28 July 1962, is an ex-GWR diesel set. A set used to run, with an ordinary coach in the middle, on the Birmingham (Snow Hill) to Cardiff via Stratford and Cheltenham (Malvern Road) express service. At the left of the picture, making an interesting contrast, is a poster for the new era Pullman Diesel Services.

T. David/C. L. Caddy Coll

On a wet Saturday in 1961, a BR Standard 73XXX 4-6-0 enters the north end of the down platform on an express and passes the station box, which opened in June 1891, presumably in connection with the arrival of the MSWJ, and replaced the one adjacent to the south end of the platform. *R. Wales*

The splendid combination of a Midland 'Spinner' 4-2-2 and a 2-4-0 pull away on a northbound express in the early years of the century. The large bridge carrying the Gloucester Road is there today and the photo was taken from the road leading down to the tram depot of the Cheltenham and District Light Railway Co., used now for buses. *J. D. Blyth Coll*

MSWJ 2-4-0 No. 12 stands ready to leave the Vineyards on a local train in 1917, these sidings having been installed especially for the MSWJ. The engine is in unlined black livery. The three 2-4-0s dispersed after the grouping, but one, in its rebuilt form, worked a railtour on its old stamping grounds from Cheltenham in 1953. *A. B. MacLeod Coll/N.R.M. York*

Looking towards Lansdown station, LMS 2P 4-4-0 No. 496 heads a northbound express at Alstone Junction in the 1930s. On the extreme left edge of the photo, the track curving off leads to Alstone Wharf. The large building in the background was the Sunningend works of H. H. Martyn, responsible for fitting out the interior of the Cunard transatlantic liner *Queen Mary* around this time.   *E. R. Morten*

A GWR engine on LMS metals moves across Alstone crossing in March 1933. Probably the freight had started just a short distance away at the High Street goods yard and was heading for the MSWJ at Lansdown Junction. The MSWJ possessed running powers over the Midland Railway between High Street goods yard and Lansdown Junction, which powers would have transferred to the GWR when it took over the MSWJ. Alstone Junction signal box on the right opened in May 1891 and is still here in 1993 as a ground frame.   *E. R. Morten*

A view of Malvern Road station, taken in 1967, after closure. The station opened on 30 March 1908 as part of the GWR's route from Birmingham to Bristol, what the Great Western Railway magazine described at the time as a new railway through the 'Garden of England'. The station had its own approach road off Malvern Road and had an island platform, with a bay at the north end which was used by Honeybourne auto trains coming in and out of St. James' station. *W. Potter*

By the middle of 1965, there was only one regular steam working into St. James', the 5pm from Gloucester (Central). This produced a variety of motive power, on 29 July being the last 'Castle' in active service, No. 7029 *Clun Castle*, which suffered the indignity of returning tender first on a local trip freight. This view shows well the up platform, footbridge and booking hall. *W. Potter*

During World War 2, the GWR had a number of LNER J25 0-6-0s on loan and one is seen shunting at the end of the down platform at Malvern Road in 1940, with a busy yard full of interesting stock. The coaling stage is prominent in the middle foreground, with the loco shed at the right rear. *J. D. Blyth*

In the post war years, 4-6-0 No. 4073 *Caerphilly Castle* pulls out of Malvern Road with a down express in April 1946. *E. R. Morten*

Nearly twenty years later, BR 'Britannia' 4-6-2 No. 70045, shorn of its *Lord Rowallan* nameplates, stands outside Malvern Road West signal box with a Saturdays only Wolverhampton to Minehead and Ilfracombe train on 7 August 1965. This class became familiar on the Honeybourne route in 1965 on summer Saturday trains, but were otherwise never very common, even on the ex LMS line through Cheltenham. *W. Potter*

GWR 'Aberdare' Class 2-6-0 No. 2673 departs from the north end of Malvern Road in March 1945, while sister engine No. 2638, allocated to Chester, sits on the back road of the loco shed, having broken a crankpin. The loco was not repaired and was still here in September 1945 when it was officially condemned. *W. Potter*

A glamorous visitor coming under Malvern Road bridge on 14 May 1960 is record breaker 4-4-0 *City of Truro* on a special organised by the Gloucestershire Railway Society. The train had just left St. James' station and was proceeding towards Andoversford and the old MSWJ to Southampton. In earlier days, GWR 4-4-0s were an everyday sight at Malvern Road. *W. Potter*

Malvern Road depot in 1949. The original shed building is on the right, with the later extension on the left. Loco 6384 still has the GWR style front number on the buffer beam, while 2-6-2T No. 5574 has acquired the BR style smokebox numberplate. *W. Potter*

After Tewkesbury shed closed, Malvern Road crews worked some passenger turns on the Ashchurch-Evesham route, with the engine coming to Malvern Road for servicing. This brought in a variety of locos, including, as shown here, Fowler 2-6-4T No. 42422 from Saltley. The driver oiling round is Chris Betteridge and at the front of the cab is Dave Rosamund. Ex LMS engines were familiar on the shed, as the High Street pilot, usually a Barnwood 'Jinty' 0-6-0T, stabled here after the closure of the MSWJ shed in 1935. *R. Stanton*

On 10 August 1962, 4-6-0 No. 4087 *Cardigan Castle* passes the site of the old loco shed and is about to go under St. Georges Road bridge and attack High Street bank with a relief train from Newquay to Wolverhampton. This must have been one of the engine's last workings, as it was put into store only three days later, although its external condition at least suggests it is good for many more miles. The lines to the left lead to St. James' station and the signal box is Cheltenham Malvern Road East – Malvern Road station is past the bridge in the background.

J. Dagley-Morris

ST JAMES'

CHELTENHAM (ST. JAMES). GWR

'Metro' tank No. 4 stands at the rebuilt St. James'. At the rear is a celestory coach, with another in the opposite platform. The loco had been put into traffic in April 1869, fitted with condensing apparatus, for working on the GWR's underground services in London. Like all good old engines, it had moved to the country to work out its remaining years on less strenuous duties. The engine was withdrawn from service in March 1913.

Lens of Sutton

A June 1947 shot of Mogul 2-6-0 No. 6341 waiting to leave on a local train at platform 4. Note the station nameboard shows just CHELTENHAM SPA without the addition of (ST. JAMES). Prominent landmarks outside the station are the Barnby Bendall furniture repository at the left, St. Gregory's church behind the engine and St. Matthew's church to the right. While these three landmarks survive today, the station itself has been demolished.

W. Potter

An overall view of St. James' station, with the goods shed on the right and a small Prairie tank standing in the platform.

M. P. Barnsley Coll

Top: One of the more obscure workings from St. James' was the Sundays only 8.20am to Bristol (Temple Meads) via Gloucester (Eastgate), for which the engine travelled over light from Gloucester. Bristol (Barrow Road) based BR Standard 4-6-0 No. 73054 is just leaving on 12 February 1961. *J. Dagley-Morris*

Middle: From left to right, guard, driver, fireman and stationmaster pose for the camera at St. James'. *R. Stanton*

Bottom: A close-up of the turntable, taken in November 1951. While it was adequate for most types that worked in, it was not big enough for larger engines, such as 'Castles'. After closure of the flat crossing at Ashchurch in 1957, tender engines, like the Midland 2P 4-4-0s, have been known to run light engine off the Evesham line, to turn at St. James'. *W. Potter*

Not long before the end of the service, U Class 2-6-0 No. 31803, of Eastleigh shed, is ready to depart with the 1.52pm to Southampton on 20 August 1961. By this date there was only one return service, on Mondays to Saturdays, over the whole route between Cheltenham and Southampton. *T. David/C. L. Caddy Coll*

Immaculate 4-6-0 No. 7813 *Freshford Manor* stands in front of the turntable at St. James' on 7 October 1962. It has just arrived on the 1.20pm express from London (Paddington). Possibly the engine has recently been overhauled in Swindon Works. *J. Dagley-Morris*

The return freight working of the 5pm passenger from Gloucester is here seen with 2-6-2T No. 4100 on 6 August 1965. The photo gives an overall impression of the yard at the St. George's Road end, near the junction with the Honeybourne line. The station signal box is on the far left and a Hymek diesel stands at the platform on a passenger train.

W. Potter

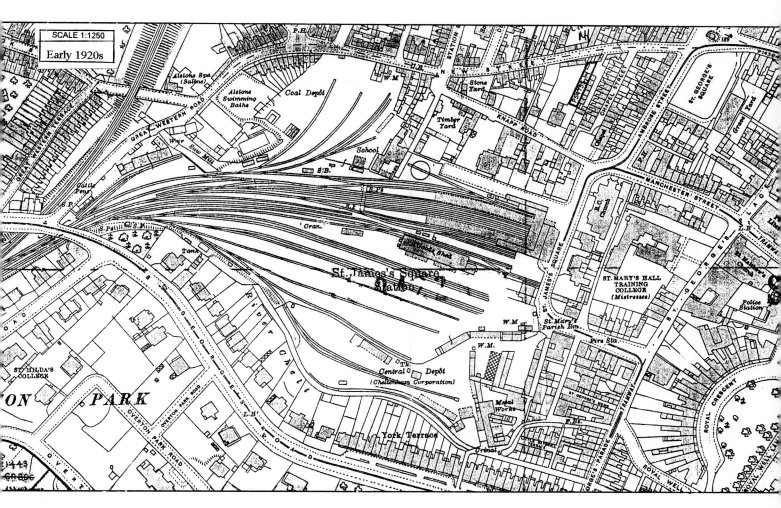

2-8-2T No. 7207 drifts past the cemetery at Market Street heading for the junction with St. James' and on to Malvern Road on 27 September 1960. These powerful tank locos worked regularly in the areas, often on iron ore and steel trains. Part of the cemetery was demolished to make way for the Honeybourne line
R. Dagley-Morris

A GWR 2-8-0 coasts out of Hunting Butts tunnel in July 1941 with a down freight. The number 1 on the loco's smokebox possibly indicates that this was part of a series of trains, no doubt some vital wartime traffic.   *W. Potter*

THE
HONEYBOURNE
LINE

This view shows the construction of Cheltenham Race Course station, looking towards the main Evesham road. The platform retaining walls are well under way and the station opened on 13 March 1912.   *M. P. Barnsley Coll*

RACE DAY SPECIALS

The essence of Gold Cup week race specials is captured here in this portrait of immaculately turned out double-headed 'Castle' 4-6-0s ready to take the punters back to London on 6 March 1961. The locos are *Avondale Castle* and *Earl of Powis*. Race specials were the only passenger trains to call at the station since the cessation of the Honeybourne auto trains in the previous year.

J. Dagley-Morris

On 29 December 1960, a grubby Gloucester 'Hall' 4-6-0 No. 5914 *Ripon Hall* arrives at Cheltenham Race Course with the 9.5am special from Paddington. This train had called at Gloucester Central and probably changed engines there. *J. Dagley-Morris*

At Southam on 11 June 1963, is the modern form of 9F 2-10-0 No. 92227 on a down iron ore train. This traffic was one of the staple loads on the line, going from the ironstone fields around Banbury to South Wales steel works.   *W. Potter*

BISHOPS CLEEVE

A distinctly rural view of the Honeybourne auto train leaving Bishops Cleeve with 0-4-2T No. 4841 on two push and pull auto trailers.   *W. Potter*

Just a week before the service was withdrawn, the Honeybourne auto arrives in Bishops Cleeve from St. James' on 27 February 1960 with 0-6-0PT No. 9727 and two modern BR Mark I coaches.
E. Wilmshurst

A rare visitor to the Honeybourne line is Eastern Region 4-6-0 No. 61083 on a Sunday diversion from the ex-Midland main line through Ashchurch, where the B1 Class was quite familiar. The train is the 1.32pm Sheffield Midland to Bristol Temple Meads on 3 September 1961 and the location is Bishops Cleeve station.   *J. Dagley-Morris*

On 18 August 1962, 'Modified Hall' 4-6-0 No. 7915 *Mere Hall* hurries north past the attractive signal box at Bishops Cleeve with a summer Saturday train.
T. David / C. L. Caddy Coll

Another photo from virtually the same spot on 14 August 1965 shows a number of differences – the signal box has closed, the signal arms have gone and the goods shed sidings and connection have disappeared. Motive power is 'Black 5' No. 45006.   *T. David / C. L. Caddy Coll*

Along the line at Gotherington 2-10-0 No. 92243 heads a mixed goods north past the closed station, which has only one platform remaining. The stumps on the left are the remains of the usual GWR trees planted at many stations. The date is 2 December 1961.
J. Dagley-Morris

About twenty minutes later at the same place is the down *Cornishman,* complete with reporting numbers and headboard, in charge of No. 5031 *Totnes Castle. J. Dagley-Morris*

Gretton Halt, looking towards Winchcombe, on 27 February 1960, with its GWR pagoda style building and wooden platform, is neat and tidy, although will only be in use for another week. *E. Wilmshurst*

On the same day, the 1.17pm Honeybourne to Cheltenham St. James' departs behind 0-4-2T No. 1424. This photo, with the church, auto train and halt, epitomises the character of the rural railway.
T. David Coll

WINCHCOMBE

The line between Honeybourne and Cheltenham Malvern Road was opened in stages between August 1904 and March 1908. There was a motor bus connection to and from railheads and this is depicted at Winchcombe station, possibly soon after inauguration, as all the staff seem to have been assembled for the picture.   *M. P. Barnsley Coll*

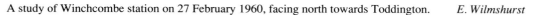

A study of Winchcombe station on 27 February 1960, facing north towards Toddington.   *E. Wilmshurst*

Empty stock for a Cheltenham Race Course to Cardiff working makes an excellent portrait in the sidings outside Winchcombe goods shed, headed by No. 7913 *Little Wyrley Hall* on 6 March 1961.   *J. Dagley-Morris*

The up *Cornishman* steams through Winchcombe with No. 5089 *Westminster Castle* on 10 August 1962, seen from the signal box window.
J. Dagley-Morris

Small Prairie tanks made a comeback in the area towards the end of steam and, here, No. 5545 shunts in a rather overgrown Winchcombe yard on 7 October 1964, with the goods shed and signal box in the background. This working was the 8.30am Cheltenham St. James' to Honeybourne pick-up goods.   *J. Dagley-Morris*

HAYLES ABBEY

No. 1424 arrives at Hayles Abbey Halt on 27 February 1960 with the 1.17pm Honeybourne-Cheltenham. A solitary passenger waits in the tin shelter. Water spilling from the side tanks on the engine indicates that it had just filled up at Toddington. *E. Wilmshurst*

Toddington yard looks busy in this view, taken in 1905, shortly after it opened. Baskets to be filled, no doubt, with local produce lie everywhere; a Beckford coal and brick merchant has a wagon in the yard – possibly traffic gained by the GWR at the expense of the rival Midland Railway's line through Beckford – and the train on the right appears to include a crane, so may be connected with the line's construction. *M. P. Barnsley Coll*

TODDINGTON

Pannier tank No. 9727, last seen at Bishops Cleeve, pauses at Toddington on the 1pm Cheltenham-Broadway on 27 February 1960. The times of the few trains which call here are chalked on a board and beneath the *Toddington* sign is a cupboard with a roller door, from which the guard presumably used to issue tickets. *H. Ballantyne*

On 3 July 1965, weary-looking 'Hall' Class No. 6915 *Mursley Hall* awaits the road outside Toddington signal box with the 11.45am Washwood Heath-Bristol freight, diverted from the Midland main line.
J. Dagley-Morris

A day later, another diverted freight, from Washwood Heath to Bristol is shown in the cutting just north of Toddington station with equally careworn 8F 2-8-0 No. 48629. Around the curve behind the train is Toddington viaduct, of fifteen 36ft spans, some 50ft above the valley floor.
J. Dagley-Morris

CHELTENHAM HIGH STREET

Many years ago, High Street boasted its own passenger station, opened in 1862 and closed down in 1910. The remains of the platform, next to the Tewkesbury road bridge, were photographed in 1947, still with a fine lamp on the platform and another one behind, which appears to be fitted to a retaining wall.

G. Lloyd/W. Potter Coll

Branching off at High Street goods yard was the half mile long line of the Cheltenham and District Gas Co. (formerly Cheltenham Gas Light & Coke Co.). From the line's inception in 1897 until 1920, it was worked by horses and by the main line companies' locos. A Peckett of Bristol 0-4-0 saddle tank (Yorktown type No. 1573 of 1920) was then purchased for shunting. It lasted until 1935, when it was scrapped and replaced by another new Peckett, No. 1835 of 1934, which features in the photograph. Taken in 1949, the month after ownership of the works had been vested in the nationalised South Western Gas Board, the loco is standing on the elevated tipping dock, where wagons were unloaded. The engine was taken away for scrap in August 1964. Remarkably at this late stage, the works acquired another Peckett, No. 2035 of 1943, in September 1964, this time an 0-6-0ST second-hand from the Port of Bristol Authority and rather larger than the previous locos. However it did little work here and went away for scrap in November 1967.

B. Roberts / J. Peden Coll

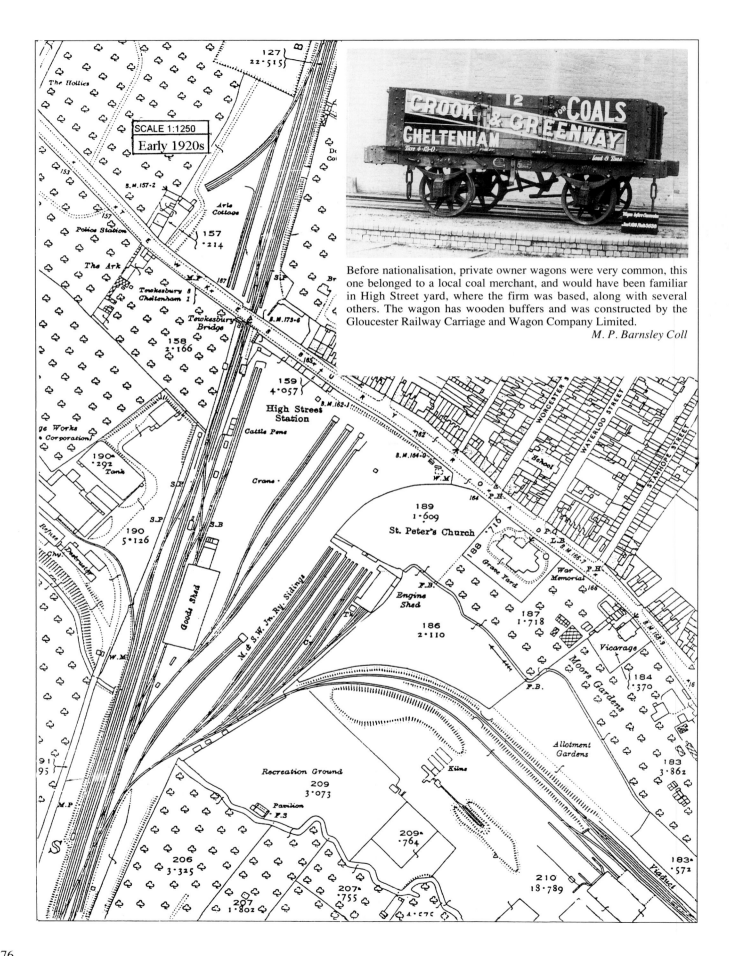

SCALE 1:1250

Early 1920s

Before nationalisation, private owner wagons were very common, this one belonged to a local coal merchant, and would have been familiar in High Street yard, where the firm was based, along with several others. The wagon has wooden buffers and was constructed by the Gloucester Railway Carriage and Wagon Company Limited.

M. P. Barnsley Coll

The Newcastle to Cardiff express passes Cheltenham High Street goods yard on 9 September 1960 in charge of B1 No. 61152 and 'Jubilee' No. 45654 *Hood*. This train was regularly double-headed, the combination in years gone by often being a Compound 4-4-0 and a 'Jubilee'. Alongside the goods shed can be seen the High Street pilot engine, a 'Jinty' 0-6-0T. The chimney in the background belongs to a council incinerator, which was rail-connected.

J. Dagley-Morris

A busy mid-morning scene at High Street yard on 22 February 1962. 0-6-0PT No. 8743 runs along a loop line, as a 4F 0-6-0 waits on a freight. A goods heading north is also in the yard, while an 8F 2-8-0 is shunting its train, possibly of coal for the gasworks and for local merchants. The goods shed, still extant in 1993, can be seen in the right background. *J. Dagley-Morris*

CLEEVE

Cleeve station, out in the country between Cheltenham and Ashchurch, was served only by slow stopping trains for passengers, but boasted its own goods facilities. The first view, towards Cheltenham, showing a couple of gangers, is undated and full of interest – the tools leaning against the parapet, the onlooker at the fence, the neat station building and the loco in the sidings. Finally, the bridge itself is of interest, as it had been replaced by a curved brick structure by the early years of this century, as shown in the second view of a down express hauled by a 4-4-0.

B. Matthews Coll

Moving on to early BR days, 25 September 1949 to be precise, finds a Wolverhampton-Penzance express passing Cleeve, diverted from the Honeybourne line due to Sunday engineering work and hauled by GWR 'Star' 4-6-0 No. 4052 *Princess Beatrice*. There appears still to be a healthy goods traffic, but the same did not apply to passenger traffic, which ceased on 20 February 1950, with goods being accepted until 4 April 1960.

W. Potter

9F 2-10-0 No. 92059 heads a mineral train past the remains of Cleeve station and goods yard on 30 October 1960.

J. Dagley-Morris

North of Cleeve was Tredington crossing and near there is depicted Class 4 2-6-0 No. 43012 on a mixed freight on 2 December 1961.   *J. Dagley-Morris*

79

ASHCHURCH

An early print of Ashchurch shows plenty of detail – Ashchurch Level Crossing signal box is situated on the up side, later the box for the crossing was on the down side. The level crossing itself goes at right-angles just beyond the end of the platform; it was double track, although may never have had a regular train service. The water tower can be seen on the left and survives to this day. An Evesham line train is visible on the right. Note also the tall signal posts.

B. Matthews Coll

On 18 March 1933 the southbound *Devonian* speeds through Ashchurch with Johnson 4-4-0 Class 3 No. 710 piloting a Compound 4-4-0. Ashchurch Junction signal box is prominent and the Great Malvern line runs off to the left. On the Evesham line on the right is a shed (possibly formerly an engine shed) and beyond is a line of railway cottages, which survive today – every other railway building in this view has been swept away.

E. R. Morten

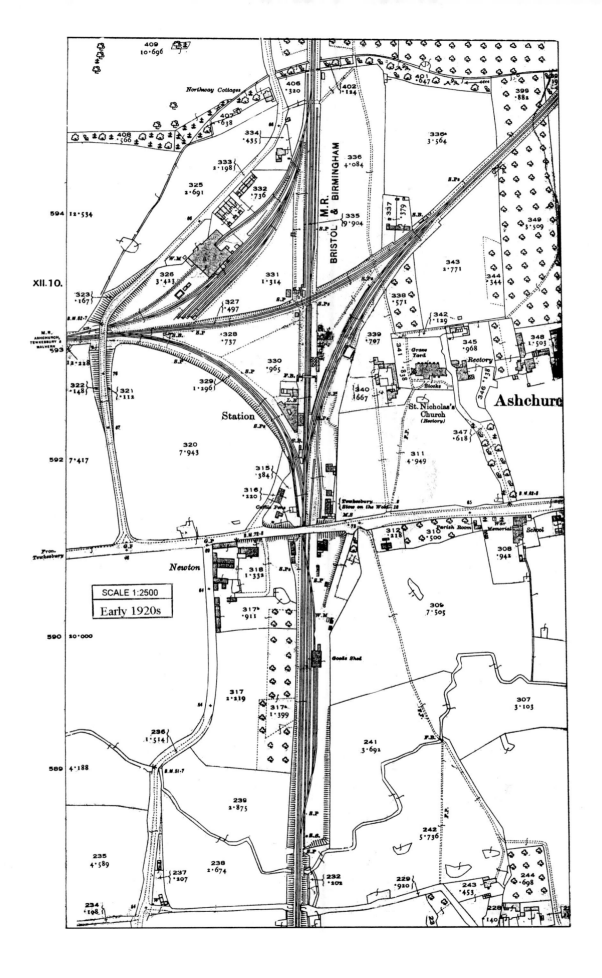

SCALE 1:2500

Early 1920s

Station

Newton

St. Nicholas's
Church
(Rectory)

Ashchurc

Rectory

Grave
Yard

Goods Shed

A post-war LMS shot, on 26 July 1947, shows a further change in motive power with Compound 4-4-0 No. 917 as pilot engine and 'Jubilee' No. 5665 *Lord Rutherford of Nelson* on a down express. 'Jubilees' were the main express engines on the route in BR days.   *B. W. L. Brooksbank*

Ashchurch on 2 April 1946 shows 'Black 5' No. 4811 arriving on a parcels train across the level crossing with the signal box, opened in October 1927. Signals for the crossing can be seen on the left, in front of the water tower and on the right of the signal box.   *B. W. L. Brooksbank*

The ornate typically Midland Railway canopy on the down side lasted for many years and is shown here in August 1963. *T. David / C. L. Caddy Coll*

0-4-4T No. M1365 (later BR No. 58063) pauses between shunting duties on 29 July 1949. The M above the bunker side number stands for Midland and was a feature of the early BR era. The engine carries turn Number 9 on the front: it left Tewkesbury shed light engine at 6am and shunted at Ashchurch from 6.15am until 11am, returning light to Tewkesbury. In the afternoon, it worked the 1.44pm passenger from Tewkesbury to Ashchurch and the 2.25pm return; went back to Ashchurch light to work the 2.50pm goods to Evesham, arriving there at 4.20pm. Departure from Evesham was at 5.5pm, back at Ashchurch by 5.52pm, before leaving with a brake van for Cleeve at 6.20pm, getting there seven minutes later. If there was any goods on offer at Cleeve, it took it back to Ashchurch at 7.41pm, then ran light to Tewkesbury shed, after a good day's work. *B. W. L. Brooksbank*

Below: The 12.30pm York to Bristol express races effortlessly towards the flat crossing on 9 July 1955, with Barrow Road's 'Jubilee' No. 45602 *British Honduras*. The delightful Midland signal at the end of the up platform sets off the scene perfectly. The straight racing stretch through Ashchurch aided many a train to maintain a mile a minute schedule over the 31 miles from Bromsgrove to Cheltenham. *H. Ballantyne*

A FEW HOURS AT ASHCHURCH

Presented here is a selection of Ben Brooksbank's photos taken between 10am and 12.40pm on 25 May 1957. These were taken only two weeks after the first major change at Ashchurch for some years – the removal of the flat crossing, which had been taken out of use on 5 May and dismantled just a week later. Otherwise things were even busier than usual due to heavy engineering work closing the Honeybourne-Cheltenham line, resulting in diversions through Ashchurch. Freight trains were being sent from Honeybourne via Evesham to Ashchurch and on to Cheltenham, but passenger trains travelled from Honeybourne to Norton Junction, outside Worcester, on the route from Oxford. This involved a change of engine at Norton Junction, where the trains reversed.

Thundering across the site of the flat crossing is a rare visitor – 'Jubilee' 4-6-0 No. 45688 *Polyphemus* from Bushbury shed, Wolverhampton – carrying a distinctive headboard for its special. These large round headboards were not uncommon at the time, one which appeared fairly regularly was the *City of Birmingham Holiday Express,* on a summer special transporting city dwellers to the seaside on day trips.

One of the pleasures of trainwatching at Ashchurch was to stand on the platform looking towards Cheltenham, observing a distant speck coming up the straight, getting even larger and announcing by the full-throated roar that a 'Jubilee' was speeding along at seventy miles an hour or more. Bristol (Barrow Road)'s No. 45577 *Bengal* hurtles past on the 8.30am Cardiff-Newcastle, in the usual splendid condition for which Bristol's Jubilees were renowned. On the left is 2-6-0 No. 43036 recently arrived on the morning passenger from Evesham.

'Black 5' No. 45056 restarts a stopping train, the 8.6am from Sheffield to Gloucester. Waiting on the Evesham line is a diverted iron ore train for South Wales, hauled by 2-8-0 No. 2887. The new Ashchurch Junction signal box is well under way, but it was to be another 14 months before it started operating and replacing the two remaining boxes, the old Junction box, seen here on the left, and Ashchurch Level Crossing box, situated on the down platform.

Here comes the diverted down *Cornishman* in the charge of absolutely immaculate Worcester-based No. 7920 *Coney Hall*. This loco came on to the train at Norton Junction, about ten miles up the line, where it probably replaced the normal Wolverhampton Stafford Road 'Castle'. Two other diverted expresses in this period of observation were hauled by a Worcester 'Grange' and an Oxford 'Hall'.

A typical train of mineral wagons, including wooden bodied examples, trundles down from the Midlands with old faithful No. 43951, a 4F 0-6-0, regular motive power on the line in LMS and BR days.

A fine panorama taken from the footbridge north of the station has 0-6-0 No. 44333 heading north on a mixed goods soon after midday. The goods in the down loop is hauled by GWR 2-6-0 No. 5382. On the left can be seen the carriages of the Evesham line passenger. The wagons in the up refuge siding are probably there for the permanent way department. Behind No. 44333, the large house with the splendid array of chimneys was occupied by the stationmaster and behind the trees on the right are back-to-back houses built for other railway employees. The old Midland provender store, with its associated sidings, by this time used by Dowty's, is prominent in the background. The flat crossing ran behind the Midland Railway water tower. In the middle background is the main station building.

Top: A 4F 0-6-0 eases off the Evesham line on a down freight on 9 October 1955.

E. R. Morten

Centre: The new Ashchurch signal box in all its glory; unfortunately it was not many years before it was superseded by more up-to-date technology, namely the centralised power box at Gloucester. It opened on 27 July 1958 and closed on 16 February 1969.

R. Stanton

Bottom: This dramatic winter photo shows 4-6-0 No. 6848 *Toddington Grange* hurrying past Ashchurch goods shed with the 10.5pm Tavistock Junction to Crewe part-fitted freight on 2 December 1961.

J. Dagley-Morris

A portrait of the Evesham line platform at Ashchurch. Around the corner, out of sight to the right, was the Ashchurch army depot, which was built in World War 2 and provided a lot of traffic for the railway right up to the early 1990s.

Lens of Sutton

Fowler 2-6-4T No. 42337 awaits departure on a local train to Evesham on 8 August 1959.

B. W. L. Brooksbank

EVESHAM LINE

The first station along the line was Beckford, just over three and a half miles away, and on 3 September 1961, 9F No. 92138 heads the 9.15am Bristol to Duddeston (Birmingham) freight, diverted from the main line, probably due to engineering works as this was a Sunday. The station building, in the left foreground, has lost the Midland canopy which it had in former days.

J. Dagley-Morris

TEWKESBURY LINE

This view is taken at the former Tewkesbury Junction, Ashchurch; straight ahead is the flat crossing line to Evesham, while the line on the right curves into Ashchurch station, where a train awaits departure. Tewkesbury Junction signal box was in the vee, but shut in October 1927. Ashchurch Level Crossing signal box is slightly left of centre in the photo. To the left of this viewpoint is the old prevender store and sidings which served it, later taken over by the Dowty Railway Preservation Society.　　*B. W. L. Brooksbank Coll*

In early BR days – 15 May 1948 – 0-4-4T No. 1371 (later BR No. 58068) stands at Ashchurch with a Great Malvern train, typically just one coach. The loco is fitted with condensing apparatus, which reveals an earlier career working through Metropolitan Railway tunnels in the London area. Now it is just another old engine put out in the country to finish its working life.　　*W. Potter*

Top: 0-4-4T No. 41900 has just arrived from Upton-on-Severn on its single coach and will run round before heading back. This view shows the buildings to good effect. In the left background is one of the Dowty Group factories. The date is 23 August 1958. *E. Wilmshurst*

Bottom: The passenger service ceased in 1961, but the branch goods survived for some time. On 16 October 1963 0-6-0PT No. 4684 arrives from Upton and Tewkesbury. Behind the train is the old Midland Railway provender store, later taken over by the Dowty Group. It suffered a disastrous fire in 1963, which also affected the Dowty Railway Preservation Society in the adjacent sidings, when a crane brought in to remove some of the damage toppled over on to a GWR saloon coach, causing extensive damage, and completely wrecking a GWR Dean 40ft. vehicle. *T. David/C. L. Caddy Coll*

0-4-4T No. 58071 trundles past Tewkesbury box towards the station with its single coach load for Upton-on-Severn on 24 September 1955. The branch line visible behind the box goes to the goods yard, the engine shed, the original terminus station at Tewkesbury and the quay. No. 58071, formerly LMS No. 1377, was the last engine in the area to retain Salter safety valves.   *W. Potter*

On the line from the quay, the original station and the engine shed, this view at the Chance Street crossing, from November 1951, is looking towards the junction with the line from Malvern, Upton and the current Tewkesbury station and on to Ashchurch. On the left is the gatekeeper's house.

B. W. L. Brooksbank

Chance Street on 1 November 1951, with the line to the original Tewkesbury station; the engine shed is beyond the malthouse, on the right.   *B. W. L. Brooksbank*

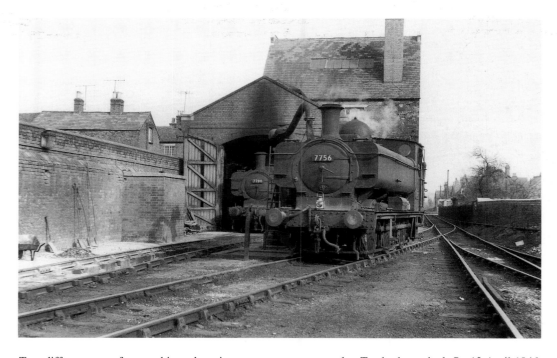

Two different eras of ownership and motive power are represented at Tewkesbury shed. On 13 April 1946, it is all LMS with 0-4-4T No. 1365 and a Stanier 2-6-2T. The latter type disappeared from the area in later years, while the 0-4-4T soldiered on until withdrawal. In the late 1950s, the Western Region took control of the area and the GWR presence is total on 11 March 1961 with two pannier tanks, Nos. 7756 and 7788. Both engines were sub-shedded to Tewkesbury from their home depot, the former MR/LMS Gloucester (Barnwood). In fact, Barnwood still had Midland engines available in 1961 and these still appeared regularly at Tewkesbury. Note that the fine Midland lamp standard has vanished compared with the earlier view and television aerials have sprouted on the adjacent houses.   *E. R. Morten /W. Potter*

The site of the original Birmingham and Gloucester Railway station at Tewkesbury, opened on 21 July 1840 and closed to passengers from 16 May 1864. The platform had been on the right and there was an overall train shed, removed in World War 2. The station offices can be seen on the right, at the end of the wall. The right-hand line runs through to cross the High Street and enter Tewkesbury quay and Healing's Mill, seen in the centre background. This photograph was taken on 1 November 1951.   *B. W. L. Brooksbank*

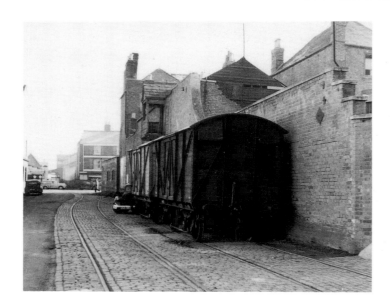

The line from Tewkesbury quay, looking across the High Street, and on to the engine shed closed from 1 February 1957; this view was taken in March 1957. The two vans stood in the old station for some years until redevelopment overtook the area. The rails are embedded in stone setts.

D. Bick

A works picture of a Healing's wagon. Healing's provided traffic for the railway for many years, from sidings on the quay branch. Wagons were worked on the quay lines by gravity, horses and tractors, engines apparently not being allowed beyond the High Street.   *M. P. Barnsley Coll*

When the terminus station at Tewkesbury closed in 1864, a temporary station was opened on the through line to Malvern. The station, shown here on 1 November 1951, was opened around 1872; trains from Ashchurch came in from the right. The station closed to passengers on and from 14 August 1961.   *B. W. L. Brooksbank*

The view from Tewkesbury station, towards Upton, in November 1951. The left-hand track was, by this time, used only for wagon storage.   *B. W. L. Brooksbank*

0-6-0PT No. 7756 awaits departure from Tewkesbury on the 11.10am to Ashchurch on 25 March 1961.   *B. W. L. Brooksbank*

Top: 3F 0-6-0 No. 43506 emerges from the 420-yards long Mythe tunnel into the sunlight on 17 September 1955 on an Ashchurch-Upton passenger.

W. Potter

Centre: Class 1P 0-4-4T No. 58059, ex LMS No. 1353, still has LMS on its tanks in this photo of 15 April 1949. It is working an Ashchurch to Great Malvern train out of Tewkesbury. The other line was used only for wagon storage.

B. W. L. Brooksbank

Our coverage of the Tewkesbury area ends near Twyning Farm and a view towards Ripple with a Class 3F on the Malvern passenger, 27 December 1950.

B. W. L. Brooksbank